D0900443

The Routledge Critics Series

GENERAL EDITOR: B. C. SOUTHAM, M.A., B.LITT. (OXON.)
*Formerly Department of English, Westfield College,
University of London*

Titles in the series

De Quincey	John E. Jordan
W. D. Howells	Edwin H. Cady
Johnson	John Wain
Orage	Wallace Martin
Swinburne	Clyde K. Hyder
Wordsworth	W. J. B. Owen

Orage

as Critic

Edited by

Wallace Martin

Professor of English
University of Toledo

Routledge & Kegan Paul
London and Boston

First published in 1974
by Routledge & Kegan Paul Ltd
Broadway House, 68-74 Carter Lane,
London EC4V 5EL and
9 Park Street,
Boston, Mass. 02108, USA
Set in Monotype Ehrhardt
and printed in Great Britain by
Willmer Brothers Limited, Birkenhead
Copyright Wallace Martin 1974

ISBN 0 7100 7982 6
Library of Congress Catalog Card No. 74-81996

General Editor's Preface

The purpose of the Routledge Critics Series is to provide carefully chosen selections from the work of the most important British and American literary critics, the extracts headed by a considerable Introduction to the critic and his work, to the age in which he was writing, and to the influence and tradition to which his criticism has given rise.

Selections of a somewhat similar kind have always existed for the great critics, such as Johnson, Wordsworth, Arnold, Henry James, and the argument for their appearance in this series is that of reappraisal and re-selection: each age has its own particular needs and desiderata and looks in its especial own way at the writing of the past—at criticism as much as literature. And in the last twenty years or so there has also been a much more systematic and intelligent re-reading of other critics, particularly the lesser-known essayists and reviewers of the Victorian period, some of whose writing is now seen to be criticism of the highest order, not merely of historical interest, but valuable to us now in our present reading of nineteenth-century literature, and so informing us in our living experience of literature as well as throwing light upon the state of literature and criticism at particular moments in the past.

B.C.S.

Contents

Preface

Most of Orage's literary criticism originally appeared in the weekly columns that he wrote for *The Labour Leader* (1895–7), *The New Age* (1913–21) and *The New English Weekly* (1932). There are over four hundred in all, few of which treat less than three or four subjects. While republication of selected columns in their original form would have eliminated many editorial difficulties, it would not have provided an adequate representation of Orage's criticism as a whole.

Working with materials accumulated during the course of a week (for example, a novel, an issue of a little review, a biography, and an article in the press), the literary columnist employs his own theories and methods to solve a practical problem: that of producing an interesting and reasonably coherent discussion of them. The resultant column implicitly embodies a duration of interest: written for a particular week, it may be worth reading weeks later (as one reads old weeklies while abroad), but its combination of subjects, determined largely by its journalistic origin, is rendered pointless by the passage of years. If republished decades later, the criticism thus produced can benefit from a different order of presentation, one appropriate to the mode of publication and its assumed duration of interest.

Ideally, a representative selection of a critic's work would accurately convey the impact that he had on his contemporaries, reanimate the issues that seemed consequential in his time, provide a balanced picture of his strengths and weaknesses, and at the same time draw attention to those features of his work that are of particular interest today. Certain sections of this volume are intended specifically to serve one or more of these functions. To wrench a critic's work from its context in the interests of posterity is to neglect his living influence while remaining oblivious to the ways in which the present conditions our conception of what is of permanent value. But in the end, the present is ill served by an exclusive devotion to literary history, since our own conceptions of history determine what we see in the past. One virtue of Orage's criticism is that although it originated as journalism, the most ephemeral of literary forms, much of it is worth reading today. When, therefore, a choice seemed to be required, I selected for inclusion in this volume passages which I thought would interest the contemporary reader, rather than those of purely historical interest. About half of those here reprinted are not contained in the three collections of Orage's criticism previously published.

I should like to thank Noel Stock for suggestions regarding the contents and arrangement of this volume.

Orage's criticism is reprinted by kind permission of the Artemis Press.

Introduction

I

From 1913 until 1921, A. R. Orage wrote a literary column for *The New Age*, a political weekly of which he was the editor. Selections from the column were republished in *Readers and Writers, 1917–1921* (1922) and *The Art of Reading* (1930); passages from these two books constitute the substance of his *Selected Essays and Critical Writings* (1935), edited by Herbert Read and Denis Saurat, which appeared the year after his death. T. S. Eliot and Ezra Pound were among those whose praise of his criticism has been responsible, if not for establishing his reputation, at least for generating curiosity about it. Orage's books are now available only in expensive American reprints, and few libraries hold files of *The New Age*. The present selection makes accessible some of the evidence on which a reassessment of his criticism might be based, and it should help confirm John Holloway's conjecture that 'when his work is better known, Orage may prove to be one of the decisive figures in the continuity of criticism over the last century.'[1]

The history of criticism shows that a weekly literary column is a fragile basis for a critical reputation. During the past century, such columns have usually been the byproduct of other creative or journalistic activities. The best-known columnists of Orage's time—Clement Shorter, W. Robertson Nicoll, and J. C. Squire—are now remembered only in histories of the period. Book reviews may prove of enduring interest, as recent collections of those by Lytton Strachey and J. M. Murry indicate, but the reviewer with an eye to posterity will prefer to write review-articles which for practical purposes (that is, subsequent publication in a book) are critical essays. The best columnist of the Edwardian period was probably Arnold Bennett, whose 'Books and Persons' appeared in *The New Age*, 1908–11.

Orage appears to have initiated his column 'Readers and Writers' (signed 'R. H. C.') in 1913 largely because he could find no adequate replacement for Arnold Bennett. Several times in the next few years he attempted to train young contributors to take over the column, helping them rewrite paragraphs that appeared therein over their own signatures,[2] but it was not until 1921 that he found in Herbert Read someone capable of the task. His letters to Read show that Orage was conscious of the limitations that the writer of such a column must impose on himself. 'Beware of the robustiousness that writes an *essay* in place of a *causerie*,' he wrote; and 'beware of too often choosing subjects *unfamiliar* to your readers' (22 and 26 August 1921). A weekly column can incorporate the sustained attention to authors and texts that we expect in critical essays only by sacrificing many qualities that make it good journalism.

In some respects, an engaging column is more difficult to write than a critical essay. 'The greatest difficulty,' wrote Orage in the preface to *Readers and Writers*, 'is encountered in the fact that literary events, unlike political events, occur with little apparent order, and are subject to no easily discoverable or demonstrable direction. In a single week every literary form and tendency may find itself illustrated, with the consequence that any attempt to set the week's doings in a relation of significant development is bound to fall under the suspicion of impressionism or arbitrariness' (p. 6). Despite this disadvantage, Orage's columns, when assembled in a form that reveals the continuities masked by the accidents of their origin as a chronicle, can lay claim to permanent significance.

As Eliot noted in *The Use of Poetry and the Use of Criticism*, 'our criticism, from age to age, will reflect the things that the age demands; and the criticism of no one man and no one age can be expected to embrace the whole nature of poetry or exhaust all of its uses.' The period during which Orage wrote is now viewed as one of transition, and changes in criticism accompanied those in literature. The great Victorian critics had concerned themselves with the relationship of literature to culture as a whole. The characteristic criticism of the past four decades concentrates on explication of individual texts or (if the term is enlarged to include the study of literature in the broadest sense) on literary history. The latter emphasis is largely a result of the growth of English studies in the universities; the former, which achieved prominence through the writings of Richards, Leavis, and Empson, originated in the criticism of Henry James, Pound, and Eliot. In viewing technique and sensibility as the most significant features of literary creation, these latter authors gave rise to a method of detailed textual analysis which has proved useful in securing recognition of their own works but which has lent itself to abuses they could not have envisioned.

By insisting that biography, psychology, politics, and ideologies provide no basis for critical judgment, Orage contributed to a recognition of the autonomy of literature, which has been one of the fundamental assumptions of modern criticism. His advocacy of textual explication at a time when many critics argued that the beauty of literature was destroyed by analysis likewise allies him with the modern tradition. But in distinguishing literature from biography and ideology, Orage did not dissociate it from life and ideas. The best of his criticism treats themes which pervade the works of Ruskin, Arnold, and Morris: the uses of literature and its place in culture during a period of social and industrial change. Orage's attempts to reconcile the autonomy of literature with what he considered its cultural responsibilities constitute that part of his criticism which is of greatest interest today.

The methods of literary analysis introduced by modern critics have become the basis of a pedagogy—valuable in itself, but uncertain (when not dogmatic) regarding its relationship to other disciplines and to culture as a whole. The writings of Raymond Williams, Richard Hoggart, Malcolm Bradbury, and George Steiner, although differing in perspective and method, testify to a renewed interest in issues that animated Victorian criticism, and we seem to be entering another period of transition, to which Orage's criticism is particularly relevant.

II

To discern that a critic exemplifies many of the tendencies of his age is to satisfy one's innate desire for historical coherence, at the risk of neglecting those particulars that account for his achievement. In attempting to explain why Orage's criticism and career remain significant, a recent writer says that 'Orage is important as a representative of a type—the lower-middle-class provincial intellectual who turned up in considerable numbers around the beginning of this century and gave a new thrust and tone to English literary life. He belongs, that is, with Wells and Bennett and Lawrence.'[3] The value of such generalization is that it suggests specific comparisons which confirm our views of Edwardian society and literary life. Of these four, three—Wells, Lawrence, and Orage—displayed abilities in elementary school that enabled them to pursue their education in one of the few ways available to them: by becoming pupil teachers and subsequently attending training colleges. But the careers of these authors show that the diversity of English literature and culture during the first three decades of the century cannot be accounted for through reference to class, place of birth, and education. Helpful as they are for an understanding of personality and individual achievement, such factors cannot be said to determine or even explain them.

The youngest of four children, Alfred Richard Orage (christened Alfred James) was born on 22 January 1873 in Dacre, Yorkshire. His parents were from Fenstanton, which lies on the old Roman road from Huntingdon to Cambridge, and following the death of his father in 1874, the family returned there to live in the home of his maternal grandmother. His mother supported the family by taking in dress work and washing. Orage attended the local non-denominational church school which had been formed some years earlier by the union of the Nonconformist and Anglican schools in Fenstanton. The curriculum was typical of its day: the morning session, nine to twelve o'clock, opened with hymns and prayers, followed by reading, composition, and arithmetic; the afternoon session, two to four o'clock, was devoted to geography, object lessons, and music.[4]

Orage's abilities attracted the attention of the schoolmaster and of his nonconformist Sunday-school teacher, Howard Coote. The boys of the village usually left school at the age of ten to work on local farms, and this would have been Orage's fate, had not Mr. Coote intervened. The latter recorded the incident in his autobiography, *While I Remember*:

> One day Mrs. Orage came to see me, soon after I had started farming [in 1883], and asked me to find a job for Alfred on the farm, as she could not afford to keep him longer at school. I at once saw my father and the schoolmaster, and we agreed that it was a thousand pities to try and make a ploughboy of Alfred; so we arranged to pay Mrs. Orage a small weekly sum to keep him at school. (p. 72.)

Mr. Coote, who had attended Cambridge, took an active interest in his education. He recalled that during the following ten years, Orage 'used to come up to my house regularly in the evenings, and I gave him the run of my books and introduced him to Ruskin, Matthew

Arnold, Carlyle and Herbert Spencer' (ibid.). The vicar and Mr. Coote taught him French; within a few years he was able to supplement the family income as a pupil teacher. In 1892, Howard Coote's father enabled Orage to attend Culham College, near Abingdon, for one year to complete his training as a teacher, and in 1893 he obtained a post at a Leeds Board elementary school.

Early in 1894, after hearing Tom Mann speak in Sheffield, Orage became a socialist. That same year he helped organize the Leeds branch of the Independent Labour Party, which had been founded in 1893 by Keir Hardie and of which Tom Mann was secretary. Soon he was lecturing for the ILP; he contributed two essays to a socialist pamphlet entitled *Hypnotic Leeds* in 1894, and late in 1895, when he was twenty-two, began writing a book column for Keir Hardie's weekly paper *The Labour Leader*.

The weekly columns that Orage wrote during the following two years constitute a chronicle and an intelligent commentary on the literature of the period. As a genre, the weekly literary column can accommodate varied aims and methods; one usually expects it to provide information about new books, periodicals, authors, and publishing, with extended discussion of a single topic only occasionally. Orage's column was of this type, and in referring to it as a 'causerie,' he evinced an awareness of the personal and stylistic qualities that the genre requires. It should approximate intelligent, urbane conversation, with the addition of such uncontrived coherence as the variety of its subjects permits, and if possible the reader's attention should be so engaged as to make him feel that each week he is returning to a discussion and a personality that he knows he will enjoy.

A few passages from Orage's column will provide a more definite impression of his personality, opinions, and range of literary reference when in his early twenties than would further description.

[Discussing an anthology of Canadian poetry:] There is much of the 'limpid sheen,' and 'effulgent beam.' There are phrases such as 'wind-vexed fields,' which make us think still better of Browning's 'wind-grieved Apennines'; and obvious imitations of Young and Longfellow in 'Thou sweet physician, balmy-bosomed night,' and 'And peace falls like a feather from some passing angel's wings.' There are transplantations of Tennyson's worst mannerisms in: 'Lakelets lisping wavelets lapping/Round a flock of wild-ducks napping.' Let Canada be itself, and give up feeble imitations of Tennyson and Byron. (*Labour Leader*, 30 Nov. 1895, p. 2.)

It is well for us to bear in mind that the poetry of convention will be one day a thing of the past, and that a few hundred years hence all rhyme will be as obsolete as head-rhyme today. (*LL*, 24 Oct. 1896, p. 368.)

William Watson's sonnets on America—beautiful as they are—affect us very little, for he feels no more than we feel, and he expresses his feelings in a language quite as inadequate as our own to express mere helpless indignation. Where he says of Helles, 'Curst who would thy triumph mar,' we merely say 'Damn them!' And for emphasis, perhaps, our expression, though less poetic, is stronger. (*LL*, 12 June 1897, p. 194.)

Orage's advocacy of free verse, though advanced for his time, cannot be related to the Imagist revolution some years later; in the 1890s, free verse meant Whitman and Carpenter. His comments on fiction were less commital than those on poetry. He praised James, Wells, Stephen Crane, and Gissing; he attempted to classify novels in terms of content and fictional technique, distinguishing between 'the dramatic method of representation' and 'the descriptive method' which 'connects the events, explains the causality, puts the reader in the wings of the stage, so to speak' (20 June 1896, p. 208); he grappled with the relationship between fiction and political action. In his discussions of realism, his political and literary sensibilities are at odds with each other: the socialist sees its documentary value, but the literary critic resents its subordination of aesthetic design to verisimilitude and propaganda.

When he stopped writing the column in 1897, Orage did not lack activities to engage his intellectual interests. A 'Plato Group,' 'in origin and effect a circle for the reception of Orage's expositions of Platonic philosophy,'[5] met weekly for some years in Leeds, and he had become a lecturer for the Theosophical Society. In 1902, Orage and Holbrook Jackson formed the Leeds Arts Club, which included in its purview philosophy and politics as well as art and literature. When they purchased *The New Age* in 1907, several writers who had lectured for the Club became contributors to the magazine, Chesterton and Shaw among them. Orage and Jackson had moved to London in 1905, intending to support themselves by free-lance journalism. In 1906–7 Orage published three books: *Consciousness,*

Animal, Human, and Superhuman, based on his lectures for the
Theosophical Society; *Friedrich Nietzsche, the Dionysian Spirit of
the Age*; and *Nietzsche in Outline and Aphorism*. He also contributed
articles and reviews to the *Theosophical Review*, but his rationalistic
criticisms of theosophy evoked two editorially-sponsored articles of
rebuttal early in 1907, and his association with the Society ended
that year.

On coming to London, Jackson and Orage had pursued their
political interests through the Fabian Society. In 1907, when Shaw
and Dr. A. R. Wallace, a merchant banker, provided them with the
funds necessary to purchase *The New Age*, Fabians assumed that its
policies would be in accord with their own. However, the new
editors soon made it clear that they would remain independent and
neutral with respect to the heterogeneous collection of organizations
that then constituted the political left. The neutrality waned after
Holbrook Jackson left *The New Age* late in 1907. The leading
article, 'Notes of the Week,' was written by Cecil Chesterton during
1907–8, with others occasionally contributing paragraphs (Orage
and Shaw among them). In 1909, Orage assumed responsibility for
the leader, which he continued to write, with few interruptions, until
1922. During these years, *The New Age* was responsible for the
instigation of two proposals regarding political and economic
organization—Guild Socialism and Social Credit—for which Orage
was one of the most brilliant spokesmen.[6] His political journalism
constitutes the major part of his published writing.

At the beginning of his autobiography, R. G. Collingwood
remarks that 'the autobiography of a man whose business is thinking
should be the story of his thought.' Similarly, it might be said that
the biography of an editor should be the story of the periodical he
edits, and I attempted to tell that story in *'The New Age' under
Orage* (1967). But this view is unlikely to satisfy the curiosity of
those who find it difficult to understand Orage's seemingly disparate
interests in politics and mysticism, and his eventual withdrawal
from journalism to pursue spiritual disciplines, without reference to
his life and personality. There has been more discussion of Orage's
life than of his writings, and an adequate biography remains to be
written. Philip Mairet's *A. R. Orage: A Memoir* (1936) recounts the
main facts of his life and includes some helpful interpretation;
C. S. Nott's *Teachings of Gurdjieff* (1961) and *Journey through This
World* (1969) describes some of his activities after he left *The New
Age* to study with G. I. Gurdjieff in 1922. Autobiographies and

romans à clef in which he appears are listed in the bibliography, and although nearly all of them testify to his charm, his intellectual abilities and his kindness, they provide surprisingly different interpretations of his motives and attitudes. The most useful brief account of his editorship of *The New Age* is to be found in 'An Editor's Progress,' a series of articles that Orage wrote in 1926. His life, in so far as he wished to record it, was his life as an editor; and few writers have equalled his assiduity in destroying letters, manuscripts, and other materials that would be of use to a biographer.

Many contemporary writers whose lives neither evoke curiosity nor require explanation have written multivolumed autobiographies, the incidents about which they are most reticent often having previously appeared in their novels. Resourcefulness in insuring the survival of letters and manuscripts has become an art—and, at today's prices, a business. Differences in attitude toward the preservation of such materials are in themselves biographical facts of the greatest importance; if correctly interpreted, they can prove more revealing than scores of incidents. Orage remarked that no single biographical method was adequate to encompass the varieties of man. Those whose lives find their complete manifestation in public action, who either do not have or succeed in concealing private experiences that seem worthy of note, require, he said, special biographical skills comparable to those of the drama critic who can divine all meaning from gesture, inflection, and manner. He cites Henry James's *Notes of a Son and Brother*—that amazing work in which James conveys his understanding of members of his family by quoting and analyzing their letters—as exemplary of the method, and then says: 'Being myself an inarticulate person and having no annals to my history, I should nominate a writer like Mr. Henry James to write my biography' (*The New Age*, 14, 722, 1914). 'No annals' is disingenuous, but the purport of the statement is clear. Orage would wish to be understood through analysis of his actions and his writings, and he often suggested that all authors could be similarly understood. Going beyond Buffon, he maintained that the man (in so far as he concerns us) is the style.

On three occasions, Orage set aside his reticence to the extent of commenting on his reading, and these comments suggest a pattern of intellectual development that might well be obscured by a detailed chronicle of his life. He mentions that he spent 'a week or so at a time' with any author that seemed worthy of attention (*NA*, 17, 477, 1915), and parenthetically remarks that 'if there is any virtue in me, I owe it to' works such as the *Bhagavad Gita* and Daniel Stephens' *Patanjali for Western Readers* (*NA*, 20, 349, 1917). In a discussion of Croce, whose influence is apparent in his later criticism, he says that he spent seven years studying Plato, and another seven studying Nietzsche; 'the *Mahabharata* I will simply leave out of my reckoning for if any work is superhuman that is' (*NA*, 14, 177, 1913). Shades of earnest Victorian advocates of self-help and self-discipline are evoked by such statements, but Orage never recommended similar habits to his readers. His discussions of education were based on the premise that interest in the spirit of play, rather than discipline, was the best motivation for learning; and his pupils remembered him as a teacher who 'hardly ever used a cane' and who 'inspired me and many of my schoolfellows with a desire for reading good literature.'[7]

Self-discipline was however necessary to one who, on completing a very poor formal education at twenty, had probably never found it challenging. During his first few years in Leeds, the stimulus of friends with better minds or wider reading than his own may have been lacking; his success as a lecturer and writer, which appears to have come to him easily, brought with it the danger of a complacent self-esteem. In selecting the intensive study of Plato as a means of imposing upon himself an intellectual discipline that he had not encountered in his education, he avoided the superficiality of eclecticism and, as his later writings show, acquired impressive skills in dialectic. But this discipline was attended by other hazards. Although his political interests may have helped keep him in touch with the realities on which philosophy purports to be based, theosophy probably had the opposite effect, etherializing his Plato with admixtures of the *Bhagavad Gita* and Blavatsky.

Orage's first meeting with Holbrook Jackson in 1900 was the occasion of a decisive change in the direction of his intellectual development. Jackson recounted the incident in the preface to *Bernard Shaw* (1907): 'You left behind you that night, or rather the next morning, for we had talked the night away, a translation of the *Bhagavad Gita*; and you carried under your arm my copy of the first English version of *Thus Spake Zarathustra*' (p. 12). Several years later, Orage wrote: 'Only one whose fortune brings him, after years of arid solitary thought, suddenly and as if by chance, into a world of thought and men such as he has dreamed of but never realized, can understand Nietzsche's emotion on first reading Schopenhauer.'[8]

One cannot help but conclude that Orage experienced this emotion on reading Nietzsche.

In place of an arduous search for transcendent truth, nihilism; instead of a longing for the One, an ebullient acceptance of the necessity of the Many; celebration of those faculties that Plato would subjugate, and a devastating critique not only of the methods of traditional philosophy, but of the concepts (subject—object, cause—effect, freedom—necessity) on which they are based. Coming when it did, the confrontation of Plato and Nietzsche in Orage's mind could not have been more dramatic. For the following seven years, Orage studied Nietzsche, and a recent writer asserts that his *Nietzsche in Outline and Aphorism* (1907) is 'a reliable hand-book of masterly compression,' the best sections of which 'are in no way inferior to, one might almost say different from, modern interpretations of Nietzsche.'[9]

Nietzsche enabled Orage to see the limitations of Platonism; and experience must have helped him realize the shortcomings of Nietzsche. Personal contact with national politics and London journalism should be sufficient to bring any idealist—or nihilist—down to earth. The speculative strain of 'Towards Socialism,' a series of signed articles that Orage contributed to *The New Age* in 1907, was to disappear from his political writings in the next three years. After 1908, his articles were pseudonymous or anonymous. His interest in spiritual matters is evident in articles written in 1911–12 and 1919–21, but they contain no signs of the influence of Nietzsche or his earlier interest in theosophy. While arguing, in opposition to Nietzsche, that the existence of the soul and of an 'intention' in the universe are necessary assumptions, he insisted that 'we are honourably bound to agnosticism' (*NA*, 8, 275; 14, 81). In opposition to Plato's philosopher king, Nietzsche's superman, Shaw's superman, and the aristocratic Samurai of Wells's *A Modern Utopia*, Orage in 1910 advocated the Christian doctrine of a nobility 'that stands in no need of public testimony' (*NA*, 8, 132). By 1913 he was advocating as a basis of philosophic judgment what might appear to be the most philistine of alternatives to Nietzsche's nihilism and perspectivism: common sense.

No criterion of judgment is more British than common sense, and Orage's criticism can best be understood as an adaptation of the values and methods of Victorian critics, whose works were the earliest influence on his thought, to the literary situation created by the emergence of modernism. But the influence of Nietzsche, if not obvious, was nevertheless profound. His agnosticism, for example, owed less to British sources than to *The Antichrist*:[10]

> Strength and the *freedom* which proceeds from the power and excessive power of the mind, *manifests* itself through scepticism. Men of conviction are of no account whatever in regard to all principles of value and non-value. Convictions are prisons. . . . A spirit who desires great things, and who also desires the means thereto, is necessarily a sceptic.

Aspects of Orage's character which may appear puzzling become understandable if interpreted in the light of Nietzsche, who would have rather influenced men's lives than their thoughts. If, as Edwin Muir suggests, Orage's personality had about it an air of conscious self-creation, together with a naturalness that would almost efface any impression of artifice,[11] Nietzsche provides an explanation:[12]

> *One Thing is Needful.*—To 'give style' to one's character—that is a grand and a rare art! He who surveys all that his nature presents in its strength and in its weakness, and then fashions it into an ingenious plan, until everything appears artistic and rational, and even the weaknesses enchant the eye—exercises that admirable art. Here there has been a great amount of second nature added, there a portion of first nature has been taken away:—in both cases with long exercise and daily labour at the task. Here the ugly, which does not permit of being taken away, has been concealed, there it has been reinterpreted into the sublime. Much of the vague, which refuses to take form, has been reserved and utilized for the perspectives:—it is meant to give a hint of the remote and immeasurable. In the end, when the work has been completed, it is revealed how it was the constraint of the same taste that organized and fashioned it in whole or in part: whether the taste was good or bad is of less importance than one thinks,—it is sufficient that it was a *taste*!

This passage extends the meaning of 'the style is the man' in a direction that proved important to modernism: Yeats's idea of the mask and the anti-self, which he derived from Nietzsche, and Pound's 'personae' or 'masks of the self' are among the best-known examples. Although twentieth-century versions of the concept can be distinguished from the conscious poses of Wilde and his predecessors, it remains tainted by an air of artificiality. Nietzsche, whose megalomania sometimes expressed itself in self-contradiction, if only to ensure that no one else could be credited with insights that might result from the antithesis of what he said, himself suggested how the mask might be the ultimate form of honesty and self-revelation. For he attacked the distinctions and value systems that follow from the assumption that man possesses a private, internal consciousness with a life of its own, independent of the behavioural self evident to others. In *Twilight of the Gods*, Nietzsche says that the spirit, the will, the ego, and free will are concepts that man has created in order to interpret reality, despite the lack of empirical evidence to justify them; there are in fact no 'mental causes' of actions. We are what we do; and since consciousness is possible only in association with language, which is by nature a communal instrument, there can be no 'private consciousness' as such (*The Joyful Wisdom*, para. 354). Thus the distinction between mask and self disappears, along with that between appearance and reality.

In implying that there was little in his personal history that would prove relevant to a biographer, Orage said less about his life than about his attitude toward it. There is a sense in which our attitudes are more significant than the experiences that befall us. Those who find their own lives immensely interesting and who attempt, through autobiography, to piece together the self through interpretation of their own motives, instincts, memories, and opinions, are *ipso facto* those whose lives have been constituted of these components. But it is possible to live differently. The most interesting features of Orage's life are to be found, like Poe's purloined letter, where one is least likely to look for them—in his actions and his thought, recorded in his writings.

As Orage remarked, 'very few biographers have been anywhere near the level of mind of their subjects' (*NA*, 22, 31). I am no Henry James, and could not in any case undertake a biography in the present context. Analysis of Orage's relationship to Nietzsche is exemplary of one kind of problem his biographer will encounter; and since that relationship is as much part of his thought and criticism as of his life, it deserves a few further comments.

Orage assimilated Nietzsche's thought so completely that it became part of his own; in the process, it was often so altered as to escape ready recognition as an 'influence' on Orage's criticism. The difference in their attitudes toward common sense provides an example. For Nietzsche, common sense is the accumulation of errors, precepts, fantasies, conjectures, and inferences that mankind has amassed in the course of history and perpetuates as a common basis of belief and action, without ever reflecting upon its total structure or its truth. It is an 'interpretation' without any correspondence to reality. But all interpretations of reality are false; and because common sense has endured for so long, there are reasons for saying that relative to any other interpretation, common sense is true. For Nietzsche, this conclusion was one among the many that constitute the chaotic labyrinth of his work, leading everywhere and nowhere. For Orage, common sense became the criterion of political and literary judgment. By excluding from the realm of common sense any conclusion not amenable to idiomatic expression, he avoided abstract and technical discussion in his own writing and in *The New Age*. Furthermore, he recognized the philosophic assumptions implicit in his association of common sense and ordinary usage. Language (to Nietzsche, a source of error) was for him the ultimate repository of meaning and value, as well as the index of consciousness and culture.

But common sense, however useful as a means of testing arguments and conclusions, provides no fixed values for judging them. In diagnosing Nietzsche's case as one in which the denial of any higher spiritual power resulted in an all-consuming egotism (*NA*, 10, 320–1, 1912), Orage reveals his own need to find some absolute beyond the variance of philosophy. G. E. Moore's concept of objective value, together with his emphasis on common sense and his lucid prose, proved attractive to Orage and other contributors to *The New Age*, but it could not satisfy an essentially religious need. For about thirteen years (1907–20) Orage remained committed to a position approximating Vaihinger's 'as if': he treated the existence of God and the soul as 'necessary assumptions,' their necessity being proved by experience, but denied the existence of any empirical evidence or compelling logic that would confirm them. In forsaking the editorship of *The New Age* in 1922 to study with Gurdjieff, Orage ended, or attempted to end, a prolonged suspension of belief which he had found difficult to sustain.

In 1924, after a year's study at Fontainebleau, Orage went to New York to teach Gurdjieff's system. His few literary activities while in America are described by Gorham Munson in the magazine *Dynamic America* (May–June, 1940). A year after returning to England in 1931, Orage founded *The New English Weekly*. Although primarily concerned with public issues, in particular the economic crisis, it soon acquired a distinguished group of literary contributors. He died on 6 November 1934.

The changes in Orage's life between 1921 (when he gave up the column 'Readers and Writers' in *The New Age*) and 1932 (when he commenced a column of the same name in *The New English Weekly*) were of no discernible influence on his later writings. His opinions concerning spiritualism in 1932 were almost identical to those that he had expressed twenty years earlier:

After years of search and research, my conclusion upon the three greatest and most important questions [of spiritualism]—survival after death, immortality, the meaning and aim of existence— is that I do not know. The worst of it is that I do not know either whether anybody has ever possessed such knowledge or even whether such knowledge is possible. I have no evidence to convince me of any of these things. In these circumstances the jubilee of the Society for Psychical Research and all the talk about spiritualism leave me cold. I have seen more, heard more, experienced more, than the majority of their members ever will; and still I do not *know* more of the only three matters that ultimately interest man.

Meanwhile the garden must be cultivated, though again, I do not know, I only feel, the necessity. And I can see no better patch, save ourselves individually, to work upon than the community in which we happen to live. There can be no doubt that society, principally our own nation, plays an overwhelming part in the determination of our mentality no less than our physique; and there is equally no doubt that just as in conditions of depression the physical health of the nation suffers cruelly, so in conditions of social injustice the psyche of the nation is distorted in at least an enormous percentage of its individuals. The result is that in an unjust order of society, practically every individual is abnormal either from consciously or unconsciously abetting the injustice or from consciously or unconsciously resenting and combatting it. Yet what is there to be done, but to try to establish justice, if only in the interest of our successors, and to try to do it without too much resentment, too much egotism and too much ambition. Without a little of each of these it is probable that no reformer would raise a finger for society. With too much he becomes a curse. It is necessary to find the objective mean between these subjective extremes. (*NEW*, 1, 262, 1932.)

Orage remained committed throughout his career to the social and spiritual interests evident in his earliest writings. The most noteworthy shift in his intellectual orientation, which occurred between 1907 and 1913, involved his methods of testing and presenting ideas. From Plato, theosophy, and Nietzsche, he had before 1907 constituted a visionary conception of the purpose of life as an evolution toward a higher level of consciousness. Mystical extensions of Darwinism were not uncommon in the late nineteenth century, as Tom Gibbons has shown in *Rooms in the Darwin Hotel* (1973); for Orage, as for Havelock Ellis and Arthur Symons, the ideal function of art and literature was to manifest kinds of consciousness that would contribute to spiritual evolution. Such a conception assumes a hierarchical ordering of awareness, and it can be extended into political theory to justify the idea of a spiritual or cultural aristocracy; it is by nature opposed to plutocracy and commercialism, which are based on material values.

By 1907, Orage had realized that Nietzsche's nihilism destroyed the foundations not only of traditional philosophy, but of all ultimate sanctions of values. He could not bring himself to accept the idea of a universe without purpose, for this would render all action meaningless; yet the only alternative would seem to be a civilization in which the purposes of the powerful were imposed upon the weak. As he discussed this dilemma in the series of articles 'Towards Socialism' (1907), a tentative answer emerged: men must attempt to agree upon a social and cultural purpose, one in accord with the possibilities of nature as we know them, for we can assess social means only in relation to a defined end; and agreement upon such an end can be achieved only through open and honest discussion.

Because most of Orage's literary criticism was written after 1912, I shall not discuss the early and transitional phases of his thought or the literary opinions he expressed during those years. They are admirably summarized in *Rooms in the Darwin Hotel*, where Gibbons places them in a context that does much to illuminate them. After 1912, Orage retained, in modified form, conceptions appearing in his earlier writings—a belief in the uniquely important function of art as the creator of new imaginative values that transcend rational thought; an animus against repertorial realism; a conception of culture and nature as constituting an organic whole; the assumption that literary judgments are meaningful only in relation to social and cultural values. The distinctive feature of his later criticism is methodological. He employs common sense as the test of his conclusions and sees the jury of mankind as the arbiter of critical opinions.

III

The selections from Orage's criticism appearing in the first section of this volume, 'Discriminations,' contain the definitions and principles upon which Orage's mature criticism was based. His discussion of how language is related to reality, culture, and reason cannot be called philosophic, in the strict sense of the term, but his emphasis on the difference between language and the reductive logical and empirical principles of positivist philosophy anticipates current discussions of the subject. Particularly striking is his assertion that words stand not for 'things' but for *'relations between things.'* Meaning is thus conceived as syntactical, rather than lexical; it emerges from process and context, rather than from static arrangements of atomic facts. Language makes the parts of culture understandable in relation to one another; in every sense, it constitutes the whole. Likewise, it can incorporate the whole of man—his sensations, his feelings, his will, as well as the intellect, which is but one of the faculties with which we apprehend reality. In making common sense and its embodiment in ordinary language the tests of truth, Orage was not so much opposing the use of reason as attempting to free it from the limitations of rationalism.

Orage viewed the reaction against reason as one of the most disturbing characteristics of his age. Some of his statements on the subject are included in 'Culture and Society,' the second section of the volume. His insistence on the importance of disinterestedness and his refusal to let ideological considerations influence his literary judgment are evident throughout his writing. After discovering Croce's classification of human activities as aesthetic, logical, economic, and ethical, he repeatedly used it to disentangle political and literary confusions. Within the socialist movement, for example, there was a tendency to identify economic with ethical considerations; outside of it, literature was discussed as if it had no relationship to economics. Some readers may prefer to pass over the definitions of economic terms included in the volume. They reflect a dimension of Orage's thought that deserves representation in any selection of his criticism, and they may help establish a consciousness of his political attitudes of which no contemporaneous reader of his criticism was unaware.

If, as Orage argued, words represent relations between things, the word 'literature' will be as variable as the texts to which it applies, and the character of any particular type of literature will result from its cultural context and function. Orage's definitions of literature and descriptions of its function are contained in the section 'Literature and Criticism.' 'On Reading' (1912) emphasizes the affective element of literature and its power to engender emotions that lead to action; a passage written in 1916 asserts that literature reveals the means of extracting truth from experience. Taken together, these comments recall De Quincey's essay on the literature of knowledge and the literature of power. Elsewhere, in discussing Milton (1913) and Sorel's *Reflections on Violence* (1916), Orage associates the 'truth' of literature with 'myth,' which attains a validity outside the limits of demonstrable truth-value. However, in a later discussion of Croce's concept of art as expression (1922), Orage concluded that the value of art did not depend on its emotional or ideational content. These statements concern the effect of literature on the reader, and all but the last involve a definition of literature that would include essays, oratory, history, and political writing. The function of literature, in the rhetorical tradition descending from oratory to other expository forms, is to teach, move, and delight. This formulation has not been improved upon, but imaginative forms require a different kind of discussion, one that identifies their intrinsic nature as well as their effects.

Orage conceived fictional literary works as intentional imaginative structures that show us what life may be or what it might become. Great literature embodies possible worlds: it is compatible with what we know of man and nature, but by representing the known as manifesting intention, it makes existence intelligible. Literature also reveals the contingency of the actual, thereby reawakening our sense of the possibilities of life. The laws of nature determine what can be, but not what is. Only by envisioning a world different from our own, yet consonant with its known laws, can we understand the potentialities of the present. Literature cannot itself resolve the philosophic problems attendant upon the assumption that the universe is intentional, but it enables us to enter a world like our own in which we experience intentionality. Given this conception of literature, realistic works—those which merely record what exists—are pointless in themselves, and pernicious in so far as they lead their audience and the literary tradition away from the true function of art. Orage's emphasis on the coherent design of imaginative literature, together with his assertion that meaning is determined by relationships between terms, can be seen as similar to the premises of structuralism. His treatment of intentionality and some of his philosophic discussions ('those old Coleridgean terms, objective and subjective, have had their day,' he wrote in 1911) remind one of phenomenological criticism.

Although Orage made use of his conception of literature in discussing particular works, he did not make it the basis of his evaluations. He claimed that judgments of literature could be true, but that their truth was established by general acceptance, not by a proof deducible from features of the work itself. Pursuing the legal analogy, he pointed out that although the critic, as judge, provided a summary of the evidence, it was the jury of mankind that rendered the verdict. The judgment thus reached concerns the literary work as such, not the author; in so far as he concerns us, the author is present in his works.

He had been present in person before the invention of writing. Orage repeatedly reminded his readers that the printed word was simply a substitute for speech, and that literary style was a means of conveying effects that in oral communication are transmitted by gesture, expression, and inflection. Man, language, and imaginative creation were originally fused in an individual, concrete presence. When writers make patterns out of printed words rather than listening to the speech they represent, and when linguists attempt to standardize pronunciation, they fragment the primordial source of the unity of literature. Orage's statements on these matters are contained in the sections 'The English Language' and 'The Literary Kinds.' They lead to another problem which he never appears to have resolved to his own satisfaction: that of the relationship between regional, national, and world literature.

His comments on language would be consonant with an encouragement of regional and dialect literatures. But despite his affection for spoken dialects, he viewed them as contributory sources of a national literary language. Literature, he said, 'takes up dialect and, after using it, restores it to speech in a purified and universal instead of a local form' (*NA*, 14, 498, 1914). Before World War I, he viewed English literature as an organic unity that could not assimilate features of other national literatures without being reduced to formlessness. After the war, however, and in part as a result of it, he became more tolerant toward the interaction of literary traditions. Literature in the English language was, for him, English literature;

but after his years in the United States, he conceded that there was an American literary style with its own tradition, deserving individual recognition. His arguments supporting statements that are here presented synoptically can be found in the section 'English Literature and Literature in English.'

Orage's views on language are consistent with his discussions of prose style. While acknowledging the varied stylistic possibilities of English, and maintaining (in opposition to the rhetorical tradition) that matter and manner form an indissoluble unity, he thought that there could be only one style that would most perfectly embody the possibilities innate in the English language. The perfect prose would not attain its effects through poetic devices, such as regular rhythm, alliteration, rhyme, and imagery. It would eschew the balanced sentences and rhetorical devices that had been the stock in trade of nineteenth-century stylists and before them the Ciceronian tradition. To the simplicity and strength of eighteenth-century prose, it would add the grace of the seventeenth century; and through it the genius of the language and its people would speak.

This collection includes Orage's discussions of contemporaneous stylists he admired, such as Belloc and Chesterton; he was not, however, charitable in his analyses of their prose. Chesterton exemplifies the writer with a unique style; it bears the stamp of his personality and by the same token delineates an area of possible subject matter outside of which it will appear inappropriate or eccentric. The ideal style envisioned by Orage would appear to be invisible; all its art would be devoted to making it appear natural, and it would contain no verbal traits characteristic of its author. Such traits 'show as mannerisms instead of being concealed and revealed as qualities' (*NEW*, 1, 93, 1932); the personality of the writer obtrudes in the sense that there is a stylistic excess, a superficies imposed upon the subject and its integral linguistic expression. His attitude toward style might simply be called neo-classical, except that he denied it involved the suppression of individuality. He said that 'to obtain to perfect originality a writer must try to write like everybody else'; the originality so described, if not anonymous, is certainly impersonal.

Orage's attitudes toward life, literature, and culture meet in his discussion of prose style. He pointed out the parallelism of style and personality in commenting on a series of articles entitled 'Man and Manners' which appeared in *The New Age* in 1916:

The perfect manner reveals the man and nothing else. His class, his circumstances, his profession, in a word, his temporal personality, are all concealed by the absence from his manners of any mark derived from them or distinguishing them. Similarly I would say that a pure style in writing reveals nothing but the thoughts and the pure individuality of the writer. His idiosyncrasies, his class, his education, his reading should all be kept out of sight. You should be able to guess at nothing concerning his temporal affairs that he does not mean to tell you. Pure style is pure mind. (*NA*, 19, 39.)

We usually think of personality, with all of its social and temporal determinants, as one indissoluble locus of individuality. Orage seems to hold that only by separating oneself from the traits acquired through circumstance and accident can one's true individuality, as a human being and as a writer, be revealed. The uniqueness thus revealed is in a sense universal. Nietzsche's dictum 'become what thou art' involves a similar distinction between personality and essential being. What prevents Orage's conception from becoming another instance of Romantic egotism is his requirement that in all externals, the individual be at one with his era; and this means, in life and in art, that he is not identifiable with any particular class. 'The dividing lines in all the arts between the major and the minor,' he wrote in 1915, 'are determined by the critical appreciation of the common people' (*NA*, 16, 313).

Critics have been impatient with the common people for over a century, and the preceding quotation, which appears in a discussion of oratory, does not adequately represent Orage's position on the subject, though it is consistent with his statement that writers are ultimately judged by the jury of mankind. The people of a capitalist society might provide a more reliable index of literary value in a different economic and commercial environment. If fault is to be assigned for their failure to appreciate good literature, critics must bear some of it, he said, and their complaints about the literary audience are unlikely to contribute to its improvement. He thought that changes in educational methods might help but doubted that they could be effected, and he recognized that the spokesmen of culture no longer commanded the respect of their audience. 'In any event,' he wrote in 1921, 'there is no use in kicking against the stars. If the forces of culture are to rule modern civilizations, they must do so constitutionally. The days of the dictatorship of the intelligentzia are past' (*NA*, 28, 259). The problems of literary judgment are multiplied when there is no common audience to which they can be referred; and likewise, the idea of a literary style without distinguishing features is not meaningful in a period in which all styles and techniques exist by virtue of difference from one another, rather than through comparison with an accepted norm. The literary and cultural norms which Orage's discussion of literary judgment posit, simply did not exist in his time, as he repeatedly pointed out. The problem of applying his principles to the literature of his time is evident in his discussions of Pound, Joyce, and Wyndham Lewis.

I have given Orage's comments on these three authors what may seem a disproportionately large representation in the present collection for several reasons. The problem confronting a critic when he undertakes discussion of a recently published book is a concrete one, regardless of the principles and historical knowledge he brings to the task. In his successive reviews of books by Pound, Lewis, and Joyce, we see Orage grappling with the difficult questions resulting from the encounter of his literary and cultural principles with their technical methods. On one occasion, he defends their innovations; on another, he accuses them of gradually becoming a coterie that alienates its former admirers, himself among them. If at times his criticism of their work seems unnecessarily harsh, it should be remembered that he recognized their importance long before most critics of his time. The critical process exemplified in his discussion of these authors does not lend itself to summary, and the issues it involves are far from being resolved today.

Aside from these selections and his discussions of Henry James, Orage's comments on particular books and authors are not in my opinion the best part of his criticism, though the excerpts in section 18 reveal his skill in poetic analysis and show that the methods advocated by I. A. Richards were not entirely without precedent. The best works of the Edwardians had been published before he began his column in *The New Age*, and many of the masterpieces of modernism were published after it ended in 1921. Many publishers, incensed by the reviews that appeared in *The New Age*, stopped supplying review copies, which fact accounts for what might appear to be glaring omissions in Orage's column. The distinction between a literary column and a book review, which he occasionally pointed out, prevented him from discussing books at length. Readers who can obtain copies of *Readers and Writers* and

C

The Art of Reading will find therein representative selections of Orage's comments on a number of Victorian and modern authors. His most significant 'practical criticism,' in the literal sense of the phrase, was his discovery of new writers (Katherine Mansfield, Herbert Read, and Edwin Muir were among those whose first published works appeared in *The New Age*) and his teaching of the rudiments of prose style to young contributors.

IV

An assessment of Orage's importance as a critic is dependent in part on one's conception of what criticism is, or should be. David Lodge, referring to Eliot's description of its function as 'the elucidation of works of art and the correction of taste,' says that 'as applied to English literature, criticism in this sense existed in a fairly fragmentary and casual form until the end of the nineteenth century.'[13] George Watson refers to 'descriptive criticism,' which can be identified with the first part of Eliot's definition, as the only kind 'which today possesses any life and vigour of its own,' the theoretical and legislative criticism of earlier periods having rightly, in his opinion, fallen into desuetude.[14] So defined, English criticism is best exemplified by the works of Eliot, Leavis, and Richards— and not by all of their works, since these definitions would exclude discussions of the relation of literature to culture as a whole.

In many ways the literary critic's recognition that he, like other members of his society, is a specialist whose discipline gives him no more authority in addressing the problems of culture as a whole than that possessed by other specialists, can be beneficial. Acknowledgment of his limitations, in addition to preventing him from speaking authoritatively about such issues as the place of literature in his society, may keep him from making certain kinds of statements about literature itself. For if statements about principles and methods entail a philosophic dimension, the literary critic must either forgo theoretical discussion of his own discipline or admit that he has no special competence, as a critic, to speak of it. The decline of English theoretical criticism in the twentieth century is no accident; it follows naturally from the assumption that the proper function of the critic is an empirical one, that of discussing one text after another. This assumption is overt in George Watson's *The Literary Critics*; it is overt in the writings of Leavis; and whether or not defended as such, it entails a particular theory of criticism.

The effects of this assumption are evident in the writings of Leavis and Eliot. In *The Idea of a Christian Society*, Eliot repeatedly points out that he is not discussing politics, or religion, or sociology, or philosophy, but something deeper which underlies all these subjects; at the same time, he admits that he could handle his own subject better if he were 'a profound scholar in any of several fields.'[15] Eliot's disavowals of competence in discussing subjects other than literature illustrate one type of limitation the twentieth-century critic imposes upon himself; the other, that of eschewing generalization, is evident throughout Leavis's writings. In *Education and the University*, he distinguishes his approach to liberal education from the humanism of Irving Babbitt by saying that 'my own aim is to deal in doctrine, theory and general terms as little as possible.'[16] The alternative, in his discussions of literature, is to concentrate attention on specific lines, passages, and works, never drifting into synopsis or historical commentary.

But Leavis and Eliot did not confine themselves to empirical 'elucidation of works of art.' Generalizations about literature in relation to culture, society, and education abound in their works; it is difficult to think of their criticism apart from their statements on these subjects, and impossible to say what such statements are to be called if not critical. Without attempting an overambitious extension of the meaning of the term, it is possible to say that the function of criticism is to mediate between literature and culture. Thus conceived, literary criticism had a significant history before the twentieth century and, for better or worse, includes statements concerning matters which are the subjects of other disciplines. This definition attempts to describe how the word criticism is generally used, rather than stipulating that it should only be used in a certain way. The dangers of conceiving criticism as a discipline that looks outward and performs an essentially rhetorical function—that of teaching, moving, and delighting a large audience in order to induce appreciation of literature—must be compared with those attendant upon conceiving it as a discipline turned inward, verbalizing a communion with literary texts in a manner of interest only to initiates.

One of criticism's mediating functions is identified in Eliot's phrase 'the correction of taste.' But the word 'correction' obtrudes; its most immediate family resemblances are with what one does in connexion with schoolboy sums, or grammar, or manners. Leavis avoids the unfortunate and perhaps accidental implications of 'correction' in his account of how sound literary evaluations are propagated. His distinction between the 'few who are capable of unprompted, first-hand judgment' and the rest of mankind, in *Mass Civilization and Minority Culture*, is perhaps a valid one. But when he goes on to say that 'the accepted valuations are a kind of paper currency based upon a very small proportion of gold,'[17] it seems that the majority are to accept the judgments of the few not because they have been induced to see the truth of these judgments, but simply because the few made them. Given our incapacities, how are the majority to distinguish gold from dross in literary valuations? Apart from the fact that the relationship between gold and paper currency is purely conventional (a fact that was generating considerable discussion when this statement was first published in 1930), it is necessary to recognize what Eliot and Leavis imply and what Orage said in 1921: 'If the forces of culture are to rule modern civilizations, they must do so constitutionally. The days of the dictatorship of the intelligentzia are past.'

In performing the most important function of criticism, 'elucidation of works of art,' Eliot and Leavis are unsurpassed. But criticism, as here conceived and as exemplified in their writings as a whole, performs a variety of functions. One of these is to maintain the precision and flexibility of language, by virtue of its relationship with literature, in periods of social and cultural change—a mediating function, in that the language of imaginative literature does not lend itself to immediate use in expository prose. Another is to assimilate advances in other disciplines and recognize changes in society so that the relevance of literature, both memorial and prospective, can be sustained and stated in terms not likely to strike its contemporaries as quaintly archaic. If the meaning and function of literature in any period is determined by its relationship with other cultural domains and with society as a whole, then knowledge of 'non-literary' matters is of crucial importance to criticism. And if, as we are often told, almost every aspect of modern society affects literature for the worse, it would be helpful to know how we and literature might more effectually affect modern society for the better.

It was in performing these latter functions that Orage's criticism was of most importance in his own time. The need for such criticism was never more apparent than in the second and fourth decades of this century, and the fact that Pound and Eliot found themselves associated, in the 1930s, with an editor and critic whose political views were very different from their own testifies to Orage's mediating position. The 1930s were marked by anomalous associations and puzzling conversions; when events rather than habits of mind drew creative writers into the public arena, the presence of critics who had sustained the nineteenth-century combination of literary, political, and economic interests was of considerable importance.

Apart from his emphasis on the importance of language, most of the ideas found in Orage's discussions of culture can be traced to nineteenth-century critics. His distinction between culture and civilization is almost identical to that appearing in Coleridge's *Constitution of Church and State*; the influence of Carlyle and Arnold is apparent in his description of culture as a passion for perfection, involving harmonious development of all of man's faculties; to these ideas he added, from Ruskin, that of the functional interdependence of culture and society. But he transformed the nineteenth-century conception of a cultural aristocracy so as to make it compatible with democracy and to dissociate it from any identifiable class. The central feature of this transformation, which does not lend itself to discussion apart from his political philosophy, was his definition of the custodians of culture in terms of function only, apart from social status or official sanction. It becomes the responsibility of the critic to induce his audience to see the truth of his judgments. The conviction that the majority of mankind is capable of discerning the truth, once it is pointed out, and a willingness to place the sanction of judgments in the hands of an audience the critic is responsible for securing, is not to be found in his predecessors or his better-known contemporaries.

The agrarian nostalgia, the resentment of machines, the wistful allusions to eras in which aristocracies (whatever their faults) had at least maintained some sort of cultural standards, which are usually part of any discussion of culture involving discrimination between better and worse, do not appear in Orage's criticism. His comments on cinema and radio fall short of the wholesale condemnation expected of defenders of culture in his time. It is possible to distinguish between critics whose attitudes toward social and cultural phenomena are determined by the *objects* and *situations* involved, and those whose attitudes are governed by the *systems* and *relations* through which particulars interact. The former praise or condemn on the assumption that value is inherent in things, and usually see changes in systems as deleterious. Orage was of the latter type in his social thought and combined both attitudes in his philosophic and critical writings.

In so far as philosophical and theoretical commitments are a part of his criticism, it suffers little from judgment by the standards of our time. Like all twentieth-century critics of repute, he said little or nothing about some writers who certainly deserved attention; and even when singling out those not commonly recognized as important, he sometimes failed to identify the particular qualities of insight and invention for which they are treasured today. The fact that he considered Dostoevsky the greatest of novelists and also wrote at length on Henry James indicates that his literary sensibility was not confined to one or another easily identifiable category. In the area of criticism least likely to secure recognition for a critic, that of expository prose, he is the equal of his better-known contemporaries, Herbert Read and John Middleton Murry.

The most important British and American critics of the twentieth century are those who have enhanced our understanding of particular literary works, authors, styles, and traditions. In his writings on literary analysis and critical judgment, Orage helped prepare the ground for the achievements of succeeding decades, but his own best criticism concerns the relationship of literature and culture to society. No one who devotes more of his time to political and economic writing than to criticism is likely to become a major critic in the twentieth century; and by the same token, no specialist in literature is likely to make the most significant contributions to an understanding of its relation to other domains of human concern. In that critical tradition which addresses itself to an understanding of culture and society as a whole, Orage's criticism deserves a significant place.

NOTES

1 'The Literary Scene,' *The Pelican Guide to English Literature*, 7 : *The Modern Age*, London, 1964, p. 89.
2 An account of one such attempt is provided by Paul Selver in *Orage and the 'New Age' Circle*, London, 1959, pp. 50–3.
3 Samuel Hynes, *Edwardian Occasions*, London and New York, 1972, p. 39.
4 Letter from Miss Eva Asplin, who attended the school in the 1880s.
5 Philip Mairet, *A. R. Orage*, London, 1936, pp. 15–16.
6 See Niles Carpenter, *Guild Socialism*, New York, 1922; S. T. Glass, *The Responsible Society: the Ideas of the Guild Socialist*, London, 1966; J. L. Finlay, *Social Credit: the English Origins*, London, 1972.

7 Letters from Charles Smith and Richard B. Kirkland.
8 *Friedrich Nietzsche*, London, 1906, p. 18.
9 David S. Thatcher, *Nietzsche in England, 1890–1914*, Toronto, 1970, p. 232.
10 *The Complete Works of Friedrich Nietzsche, vol. 13: The Antichrist*, London, 1911, pp. 209–10.
11 Edwin Muir, *An Autobiography*, London, 1954, pp. 172–4.
12 *The Complete Works of Friedrich Nietzsche, vol. 10: The Joyful Wisdom*, London, 1910, pp. 223–4.
13 'Literary Criticism in England in the Twentieth Century,' *History of Literature in the English Language*, ed. Bernard Bergonzi, London, 1970, vol. 7, p. 364.
14 *The Literary Critics*, London, 1964, pp. 9–18.
15 Reprinted in *Christianity and Culture*, New York, 1949, p. 5.
16 London, 1948, p. 17.
17 Revised version appearing in *Education and the University*, London, 1948, p. 143.

Note on the Text

Orage exercised an author's prerogative in altering passages from his literary column for republication in book form. The texts in this volume are those of the earliest printed versions. Deletions are marked with dots, except for the omission of the names of publishers and prices, which he normally listed, and the occasional omission of a 'therefore' or 'however' in the first sentence of an extract. The only other changes are in matters of convention, such as the use of italics, capitals, and quotation marks.

At the end of each selection, the source is noted in parentheses. Because nearly all are from Orage's column 'Readers and Writers,' which appeared in *The New Age* and *The New English Weekly*, I have abbreviated notation of these sources, listing only the initials of the periodical, volume number, page, and date (for example, *NA*, 13, 297, 1913.) If the selection is not taken from 'Readers and Writers,' its title is noted. Orage's occasional column entitled 'Unedited Opinions' was in dialogue form, the alternation of speakers being indicated only by the alternation of paragraphs; quotation marks have not been added to the selections from this column here reprinted.

Discriminations

Most of the following passages from Orage's column 'Readers and Writers' appeared between 1916 and 1919. Although not given to disquisitions on theory and method, Orage would occasionally devote a few paragraphs to matters of principle in discussing a book or an article in the press. Those reproduced in this section provide a picture of the concepts on which his mature criticism was based.

Orage's assertion that language (rather than a simpler set of logical principles derived from it) is the only instrument adequate for philosophic and cultural judgment is discussed in the Introduction. In connexion with his comments on what is today called popular culture, see section 11.

'C. R. A.' [in *The New Statesman*] discriminates between the handling of practical material things and the handling of words, as if the latter were necessarily 'artificialities, the imperfect verbal representations of things.' Needless to say (or perhaps it is not!) that in so far as words are properly used they do not, it is true, rank with things, nor are they even 'imperfect representations of things,' but they stand for the *relations between things*. Your practical, wordless brain deals ably enough, no doubt, with facts, and can relate fact to fact in a practical way. But a new kind of fact enters with the use of words, namely, the kind that consists not of material facts themselves, but of the relations between them. Words, that is, express the table of affinities among facts exactly as a genealogical chart expresses the affinities among a group of people. . . .

Practical men in a practical time such as the present are naturally disposed to turn upon men of words and to revenge themselves for their habitual subordination by contrasting their present indispensability with the assumed superfluousness of mere men of letters. But not only will this mood pass, but it rests upon assumptions which could only be true if men were nothing more than accomplished animals. I respect the engineer and the shipbuilder—every good workman of one trade respects the good workmen of every other trade—but, at the end of it all, what more is an engineer than a marvellous beaver? To discover, not more and more things, but more and more the truth or the real relations of things, is, on the other hand, what distinguishes men from animals. Man, in short, is the truth-seeking creature; and any material function, however ingeniously discharged, is properly subordinate to this, his unique research. But words, say what 'C. R. A.' pleases, are the tools of this trade. Words are to truth what raw materials are to any industry— the substance upon which and with which the directing mind must work. True enough that they are most readily susceptible of error, and that few minds can deal with them with precision. But the effort must not be given up on that account. Rather, indeed, it behoves us to be a thousand times more critical. And, again, it is not as if we can ever dispense with words, good, bad, or indifferent. A democracy is governed by words: all human government, in fact, is logocracy. To the extent, therefore, that the use of words is properly understood, government, even in the most practical affairs, is itself good. What, for instance, have practical men not had to pay for the failure of our intelligentsia to impress upon the public the distinction between Equality and Identity, Liberty and Doing as One Pleases, Impartiality and Neutrality? To belittle the right use of words, with the results of their wrong use before our eyes, is to invite still worse practical confusion. The only cure for intellectual dishonesty is intellectual honesty. (*NA*, 18, 421, 1916.)

2 Culture, Disinterestedness, and Intelligence (1918)

Culture I should define as being, amongst other things, a capacity for subtle discrimination of words and ideas. Epictetus, it may be remembered, made the discrimination of words the foundation of moral training; and it is true enough that, at bottom, every stage of moral progress is indicated by the degree of our perception of the meanings of words. Tell me what words have a particular interest for you, and I will tell you what class of the world-school you are in. Tell me what certain words mean for you, and I will tell you what you mean for the world of thought. One of the most subtle words—one of the many key-words of culture, in fact—is that word simplicity, to which I have just referred. Can you discriminate between natural simplicity and studied simplicity, between Nature and Art? In appearance they are indistinguishable; but, in reality, they are worlds or æons apart. Whoever has learned to distinguish them is entitled to regard himself as on the way to being cultured. Originality is another key-word; and its subtlety may be suggested by a paradox which was a commonplace among the Greeks; namely, that the most original minds strive successfully to conceal their originality. Contrast this counsel of perfect originality with the counsels given in our own day, in which the aim of originality is directed to appearing original—you will be brought, thereby, face to face with still another key-idea of culture—the relation of appearance to reality. All these exercises in culture are simple, however, in comparison with the master-problem of 'disinterestedness.' I know no word in the English language more difficult to define or better worth attempting to define. Somewhere or other in its capacious folds it contains all the ideas of ethics, and even, I should say, of religion. The *Bhagavad Gita* (to name only one classic) can be summed up in the word. Duty is only a pale equivalent of it. I mention it here because it has lately been often referred to by one or other of my colleagues, and to direct attention even more closely to it. Whoever, I venture to say, has understood the meaning of 'disinterestedness' is not far off understanding the goal of human culture. (*NA*, 23, 28, 1918.)

Pure intelligence I should define as displaying itself in disinterested interest in things; in things, that is to say, of no *personal* advantage, but only of general, public or universal importance. Interest (to turn the cat in the pan for twice) is the growing end of the mind; and its direction and strength are marked by a motiveless curiosity to know: it reveals itself, while it is still active, as a love of knowledge for its own sake. Later on, of course, it often appears that this motiveless love had a motive; in other words, the knowledge acquired under its impulse is discovered in the end to 'come in handy,' and to have been of use. But the process of acquiring this knowledge is, for the most part, indeliberate, unaware of any other aim than that of the satisfaction of curiosity; utility is remote from its mind. This is what I have called disinterested interest; and it is this free intelligence of which it appears to me that there is a diminishing amount in our day. . . .

To what is due this decline amongst us of free intelligence? There are several explanations possible, though none, I think, is wholly satisfying. It can be attributed, if we please, to the industrialization of our own country, a metamorphosis of occupation which has been longer in being in England than anywhere else. The economic balance between primary and secondary production, to which reference has been made by my economic colleagues, has been for a longer period lost in this country than elsewhere; with the consequence that we have been the first to exhibit the effects of over-industrialization in the loss of the free intelligence associated with primary production. The other nations, however, will follow suit as the same metamorphosis overtakes them. Another explanation that can be suggested is the reaction against the intellectualism of the nineteenth century. I need not dwell upon a familiar topic; but it is obvious that if faith is lost in the ultimate *use* of intelligence men become cynical in regard to the passion itself. Let us suppose that every love-affair always and invariably ended in disappointment or disaster. Let us suppose that it became the accepted belief that such would always be the case. Would it not soon become fashionable to nip the first stirrings of love in the bud and to salt its path whenever its shoots began to appear? The nineteenth century reached its climax in a vast disappointment with science, with the

intellect, with intellectualism. The fifth act of the thrilling drama
inaugurated after the French Revolution closed in utter weariness
and ennui. It was no wonder that the twentieth century opened in a
return to impulse and in a corresponding reaction from intellectu-
ality. That the reaction has gone too far is the very disease we are
now trying to diagnose; for only an excessive reaction towards
impulse and away from thought can account for the poverty of free
intelligence. Sooner or later, the pendulum must be set free again;
if not in this country, then in America, or in some of the countries
whose rebirth we are now witnessing. It cannot be the will of
God that free intelligence should be extinguished from the planet;
the world, somehow or other, must be made safe for intelligence as
for democracy.

My last guess at the origin of the phenomenon is the decline of
the religious spirit. It is needless to remark that I am not referring to
the activity of the churches. Religion, I conceive, is the study and
practice of perfection; and it is summed up for me in the text: 'Be
ye perfect, even as your Father in Heaven is perfect.' This impossible and infinite aim includes, as a matter of course, the employment and development of intelligence as one of the most powerful
aids to perfection. Fools, the Indian Scriptures inform us, can enter
heaven; but only wise men know how to stay there. And if the
perfection we seek is to be lasting and incorruptible, it is certain
that an infinite amount of intelligence will be necessary to its
accomplishment. The loss of the belief in the perfectibility of the
human spirit: in the religious duty of perfection—might easily
account for the diminution of our regard for one of the chief
instruments of perfection, namely, intelligence. Why should we
strive to set the crooked straight, since it is not only impossible but is
no duty of ours? And why labour with the instrumental means when
the end is of no value? As I have said, however, none of these
explanations really satisfies me. (*NA*, 23, 429, 1918.)

3 Rationalism and Reason (1917, 1918)

To be rational and to be rationalistic are two different things. The one is a fact, the other is a theory. Rationalism as a theory implies the sole validity of reasoning as a means to truth. To be rational, on the other hand, implies only the use of reason without setting up any theory of its exclusive validity. . . . In a word, what distinguishes rationalists from rational men is their intellectual monomania exhibited in their refusal to employ, countenance or recognize any other instrument of knowledge save formal reason. (*NA*, 21, 408, 1917.)

Coherency being the state of well-being of the mind, the mind is naturally disposed to try to attain to it. Coherency consists in the harmony of the reports of all the mental faculties, of which reason as defined is one. The effort of the mind is, therefore, quite properly dedicated to harmonizing the report of reason with the reports of the rest of the faculties. So far so good. Unfortunately, however, this effort is as painful as it is slow, for as far as reason based on observation and deduction can at present go, its conclusions are irreconcilable with the reports delivered to the mind by the other faculties. What is then to be done? The reasonable thing is to have patience, to deny none of the reports of the other faculties, because as yet, they do not harmonize with the report of reason as defined, and to suspend final judgment until complete harmony has been established, until, in short, the brain and the heart are of one mind. That, I contend, is the reasonable thing to do; and the name of this attitude of mind is in my vocabulary common sense. But the rationalistic thing to do, on the other hand, is something different— hence my quarrel with rationalism. For rationalism, demanding, like reasonableness, to have coherency or a harmony of reports in the mind, is not satisfied, like common sense, to wait until it can be brought about, but peremptorily calls upon the rest of the faculties to submit to reason as defined under penalty of being dismissed as false news-bearers. Rationalism thus arises from an impatience with reason provoked by the slowness with which reason arrives at harmony with the perceptions of the other faculties. And its revenge upon itself is to declare that the rest of the faculties are liars or dreamers. (*NA*, 21, 529, 1917.)

Another caution to remember is that reality cannot be grasped with one faculty or with several; it requires the whole. Only the whole can grasp the whole. For this reason it is impossible to 'think' reality; the object of thought may be reality, but all reality is not to be thought. Similarly, it is impossible to 'feel' or to 'will' or to 'sense' reality completely. Each of these modes of experiencing reality reports only a mode of reality, and not the whole of it. It follows, in consequence, that before we can say certainly that a thing is true— before, that is, we can affirm a reality—it must not only think true, but feel true, sense true, and do true. The pragmatic criterion that reports a thing as true because it works may be contradicted by the intellectual criterion that reports a thing as true because it 'thinks' true; and when these both agree in their report, their common conclusion may fail to be confirmed by the criterion of feeling that reports a thing to be true only when it 'feels' true. It is, I believe, from an appreciation of the many-sided nature of truth, and, consequently, from an appreciation of the many faculties required to grasp it, that the value set by the world on common sense is derived. Common sense is the community of the senses or faculties; it is, in its outcome, the agreement of their reports. A thing is said to be common sense when it satisfies the heart, the mind, the emotion, and the senses; when, in fact, it satisfies all our various criteria of reality. Otherwise a statement may be logical, it may be pleasing, it may be practical, it may be obvious; but only when it is all is it really common sense. (*NA*, 22, 502, 1918.)

D

4 Common Sense (1917, 1915)

Common sense in my personal vocabulary is something as far removed from the common as the centre of the world of thought from the circumference. What I imply by it is a grip upon reality which never weakens even when the substance under one's hand is of the very thinnest. In the simplest form I should say that common sense is the successful resolution of the mind to hold nothing as true that is not implicit in the common mind. John Smith is in my conception of common sense the criterion of truth. By what ever road thought travels, and however gorgeous may be the intellectual scenery on the way (and I like as much as any one to be intellectually entertained en route), I require that when it reaches home it shall really find itself at home. Its golden wings when they are at rest shall show the marvellous bird that has sailed the empyrean to be, after all, a bird of the earth, a home-bird; and all the truths which shone as it flew and which in its flight it sang should reveal themselves as truisms. The brilliant common sense to which I have often referred as the ambition of *The New Age* is not, in my interpretation, the discovery of anything new: it is the rediscovery of what everybody knows but needs to be reminded that he knows. Its method may be difficult; the processes of rediscovery may be complex; but, in the end, its results are, as it were, foregone conclusions, conclusions to which, implicitly if not explicitly, the common mind had already come. . . .

The absence of common sense is not, therefore, by any means incompatible with power of mind; power of mind is, indeed, very often the cause of the lack of common sense; for it is easy enough for a mind to arrive at common sense conclusions when it has not the power to arrive at conclusions of its own. But it is much more difficult for an extraordinary mind to be ordinary. My own rule in the matter is simple. It consists in requiring of every conclusion to which I am brought that it shall be *susceptible* of being expressed in what is called plain language, that is, in idiom. I do not care, mind you, in what form the thinker leaves the impression of his thought; it may be in the form of a play by Shakespeare, a dialogue by Plato, a poem by Milton, an essay by Swift, an epic by Homer or Vyasa, or a system of philosophy by Thomas Aquinas. The richer the expression, in fact, the more dignity is lent to the conclusions. But when the conclusions are examined that are contained within the expression, they should be, as I have said, susceptible of being expressed in idiomatic terms. At bottom, it is obvious that all expressed thought is addressed to the jury of mankind and is (if Mr. Durran will permit me to say it) a species of advocacy. The intention of convincing the jury of mankind that such and such a conclusion is correct or such another conclusion incorrect may not be openly affirmed by the advocate; it may not even be deliberate and explicit in his own mind; but nevertheless, it is present and operative, and I have no kind of doubt that every published work of thought is propagandist consciously or unconsciously. But this bears again upon what I have been saying, namely, that every piece of work should reduce to a simple truth capable of being understood by the jury of mankind. For what is the use when addressing a jury whose verdict in your favour you desire, of arriving at a conclusion to which, if even they understood it, they could not assent? The greatest writers and thinkers, I affirm, have always the jury of mankind in their minds as not merely the auditors but as the assessors of the case being put before them. To be sure, the greatest thinkers have also thoughts upon which it is impossible for common sense to pass judgment to-day; thoughts which it is perhaps not yet possible to reduce to truisms. But these, in my experience, the greatest thinkers carefully refrain from putting forward as conclusions; they leave them as myths, as guesses, as poetry or what not. Such, however, of their conclusions as *can* be expressed in plain terms always turn out to be the conclusions of common sense; and by that test they stand. (*NA*, 21, 448–9, 1917.)

What we mean by brilliant common sense is, in the sphere of literature in particular, a happy union of simplicity with complexity—of simplicity of form (which includes everything definable) with complexity of meaning (which includes everything spiritual and indefinable). (*NA*, 17, 133, 1915.)

5 Intuition and Idiom (1919)

It will possibly sound nonsense to affirm that the greatest books are
only to be grasped by the total understanding which is called intui-
tion; but as an aid to the realization of the truth, we may fall back
upon the final proofs of idiom and experience. Idiom, as I have
often said, is the fruit of wisdom on the tree of language; and experience, of course, is both the end and the beginning of idiom.
What more familiar idiom is there than that which expresses the
idea and the experience of reading a book 'between the lines'; for
what, in fact, is not there in the perception of our merely logical
understanding? And what, again, is more familiar than the experience of 'having been done good' by reading a great, particularly
a great mystical or poetic work, like the Bible or Milton; still more,
by reading such works as the *Mahabharata*. Idiom and experience
do not deceive us. The 'subconscious' of every great book is vastly
greater than its conscious element; as, indeed, the 'subconscious' of
each of us is many times richer in content than our conscious minds.
Reading between the lines, resulting often and usually in a total
betterment difficult to put into words, is in reality intuitional reading; the subconscious in the reader is put into relation with the
subconscious of the writer. Deep communicates with deep. No
'interpretation' of an allegorical kind need result from it. We may be
unable indeed to put into words any of the ideas we have gathered.
(*NA*, 25, 102, 1919.)

6 Culture and Civilization (1916, 1921, 1913)

To Mr. Arthur Christensen . . . I owe the definition of two ideas formerly a little nebulous. . . . Culture is interior development, while civilization is external development. Culture is thus, if I may elaborate, civilization turned inwards; civilization, on the other hand, is culture turned outwards. All that exists without or is created by the art of man has for its *value*, and hence for its criterion, the results it enables the soul to produce within. But this inner development has, in its turn, to submit to the criterion of the outer values, since natures are not finely touched save to fine issues. (*NA*, 18, 253, 1916.)

Culture is always called upon to sacrifice popularity and, usually, even its existence, in the interests of civilization, for civilization is, as it were, the child of culture, and has in general as little consideration for culture as a human child for its own education. The custodians of culture (meaning by this the disinterested pursuit of human perfection) are the adults of the race of which civilization is the children's school; and, unfortunately or fortunately, in these democratic days, their function is largely under the control of their pupils. Gone are the times when a Brahmanic caste can lay down and enforce a curriculum of education for its civilization. Modern civilizations believe themselves to be, and possibly are, 'old enough' to exercise their right of selecting their teachers. It cannot be said, as yet, that they exercise their choice with remarkable discretion; but the process of popular self-education, if slow, may at any rate be expected to be sure. In any event there is no use in kicking against the stars. If the forces of culture are to rule modern civilizations, they must do so constitutionally. The days of the dictatorship of the intelligentzia are past.

There are two kinds of judgment which it is essential for civilization to acquire: judgment of men and judgment of things. Things, it is true, are of primary importance, but so also are persons. One is not before or after the other. For instance, culture itself is a 'thing' in the philosophic sense; that is to say, it is a reality in the world of ideas; but of quite equal importance in our mixed world of ideas and individuals (the abstract and the concrete) are the actual persons and personalities claiming to embody and direct culture. Hence the transcendent importance of criticism next to creation in both spheres: criticism of personalities and criticism of 'works.' The mistaking of a little man for a great man, or the reverse, may easily mean the delay of the work of culture for whole generations. In fact, there is over-abundant evidence of it. And, equally, the confusion of the objects of culture with the objects of civilization may spell the ruin of a nation. I am afraid that few critics realize the magnitude and responsibility of their function, or the degree to which personal disinterestedness is indispensable to its fulfilment. Holding the office of inspectors of the munitions of culture, they are often guilty of 'passing' contraband upon the public, and, still more often, of failing to ensure delivery of culture's most effective weapons. More seriousness is needed, very much more, in matters of criticism. We must be capable of killing if we are to be capable of giving life. (*NA*, 28, 259, 1921.)

[Prose] is the register of culture, marking the degree to which culture has affected its surrounding civilization. Prose without poetry is impossible; and the greatest prose presupposes the culture of the greatest poetry. (*NA*, 28, 272, 1921.)

The mass of us take, even in private, serious things seriously without a suspicion that serious things are serious only because they are taken seriously. The valuation of phenomena is, after all, the only contribution men can make to creation; it amounts, in fact, to creation. Our scale of values is thus the measure of our intelligence and will—of our creative power, in short. (*NA*, 13, 573, 1913.)

Culture and Society

'Have any of my readers heard of Croce—Benedetto Croce?' wrote Orage on discovering *Philosophy of the Practical* in 1913. 'If so, they have done me and *The New Age* an injustice in not communicating the fact; for Croce is, if I am not mistaken, the philosopher of *The New Age*' (*NA*, 14, 177). What Croce provided was a classification of thought and action—the aesthetic, logical, economic, and ethical —through which the cultural and social aims of the magazine could be unified. While insisting on the autonomy of conceptual domains, Orage attempted to illustrate their interdependence, as is evident in the following selections.

The economic and political doctrines of Guild Socialism, which served as the focus of *The New Age*'s policy from 1913 to 1918, were reflected in Orage's criticism. Radical in his politics, Orage often appears to be conservative in discussions of literature and culture; the same was true of other contributors to *The New Age*. The issues involved in this seeming discrepancy are too close to criticism to be dismissed, and too complex to resolve in this context; they are at least represented in this section.

For Orage's ideas about the relationship between education and culture, inadequately represented herein, see also *NA*, 14, 308; *NA*, 20, 349 and 446; *NA*, 22, 12.

7 Reason, Science, and Culture (1932, 1921, 1915)

In America, as here, the last quarter of a century has witnessed a movement of hostility towards reason, disguised, once again in the typically neurotic form, of an objection to 'highbrows.' Because 'highbrows' profess to reason, therefore all reason is 'high-brow.' At bottom, of course, it is the objection of the school-boy to school. On the other hand, the worst of it is that the unwillingness of the school-boy is so frequently soundly reasonable; that is to say, it is sane and healthy. How are we going to distinguish between reasonable reason and unreasonable reason or high-browism? To make this distinction clearly and even popularly, appears to me to be of considerable importance in these days. And it is not to be made, I think, by simply setting science over against feeling. Sir Josiah Stamp, for example, appealed at the Colston Research Society the other day for a revival of belief in intelligence defined as 'the application of scientific methods to a continually widening area of human experience.'. . . The very definition of the scientific method is exclusive of its application to *all* 'ever-widening fields of human experience,' but confines it to some only, and those, by no means, as yet, the most important. I suggest—and not hesitantly if briefly—that the reason implied in the definition of the scientific method is only *one* of the forms of reason whose entire sum, when made up, constitutes human reason proper; and that it, too, like any other faculty in man, must be subject to the sovereignty of the whole on peril of creating a neurotic dictatorship or an equally neurotic servility.

The truth is being popularly expressed to-day in the demand not for reason, as it has come to be understood, but for men. It always happens that when reason is despaired of, the fault is men's, and primarily, of course, of the representatives of the current reason. . . . But equally there is no doubt among sane people that these experts have sacrificed the whole of reason to one faculty of reason. As the majority of people have no skill in definition and cannot put their finger on what is deficient in the reasoning of the experts, they have no means of objection but to appeal for men in place of them. Like the old lady who comforted herself with the thought that there was One Above Who would see that Providence didn't go too far, the people to-day call for men to see that the financial experts do not go too far. It is the same thing as calling upon the whole reason to see that one of its parts, namely scientific reason, doesn't destroy us. (*NEW*, 1, 189, 1932.)

Not nearly so much *mind* has been put into culture during the last fifty years as into the concrete sciences. Culture as a passion for perfection ceased to exist as a popular ideal some fifty years ago, about the time, in France, of the Franco-Prussian war. From that time forward the concentration of French intellectual energy was in the direction of physical science. France was psychologically conquered by Germany and assimilated in Prussian mentality. No doubt there were a few thinkers and artists who refused to worship the new gods; but, on the whole, the drift of the tide was away from culture; and exactly as women now are left practically alone to fill our churches, so, in general, culture in France and elsewhere fell into the hands of women. The blame, in other words—if blame there be—is upon men. The praise is women's—for having attempted to hold the pass which men had sold. (*NA*, 28, 296, 1921.)

The neglect to read widely and to think seriously upon such 'dull' subjects as history, foreign affairs, economics, etc. is often claimed as a proof of æsthetic fastidiousness instead of being accepted as evidence of narrow-mindedness. The lesser artists, the greater philistines and the man in the street, are usually at one in this. What the two latter classes for sheer brain idleness cannot study, the former class, on the pretence that such reading ruins their art, will not study; with the general result that England is in control of an Empire of which the vast majority of her inhabitants know next to nothing of how it was acquired, how it is managed and what ought to be done with it. I would not myself make instruction in these things compulsory upon anybody, even upon the gaudy radical who fancies he can govern the Empire in his ignorance. But I would silently do two things for him and for the other babes of his class. One, I would deny to him the right to open his mouth upon public affairs without having it shut by derision; and, two, I would support the small class, that has taken the trouble to earn an opinion, in carrying it out without reference to the unearned opinions of the lazy many. But per contra—per contra. Students of these 'dull' subjects are often as narrowminded as those who neglect them. There are, I understand, readers of *The New Age* who skip everything but the 'Notes of the Week' and the other political articles, on the ground that we other fry have no business poking our interests into their exalted affairs. Well, let me tell them that I despises of 'em! If I and others of us, people of letters and the arts, can school ourselves to nod at economics and politics, the masters of the latter ought not to be too conceited or idle to become in turn pupils at our school. The sooner the whole of *The New Age* is regarded as more important than any of its parts the better. (*NA*, 16, 313, 1915.)

8 The Autonomy of Conceptual Domains (1913, 1914)

In an 'Appendix to the Prophetic Books' Blake sets out in the form of propositions his formal philosophy. I am the more interested in it from the fact that it is nearly identical with that of Benedetto Croce. Croce, as I said last week, appeared to me at first sight to be the philosopher of *The New Age*. In other words, he has made explicit most of what we have left implicit or only insufficiently explicit in our criticisms. This judgment a second reading of *The Philosophy of the Practical* confirms, though with qualifications. In his main classifications of the activity of the Spirit—Æsthetic, Logical, Economic and Ethic—I personally find myself born to agree with him. If it is any confirmation of a fundamentally individual discovery I may even say that I discovered the classification for myself long ago. And here in Blake the same main outlines are to be seen. The order of the theoretic activities of the Spirit are from æsthetic perception to logical or reasoning perception; and these two comprehend what we call understanding. The order of the practical activities of the Spirit, depending on the two first, are from economic (or utilitarian) to the ethic (or moral), and these together comprehend the Will. Thus Understanding and Will are all there is to be known of the nature of the Spirit. They exhaust all the possibilities of Spirit and beyond them there is nothing. So far Croce. Blake's 'Appendix,' as I say, goes over the same ground and arrives at the same conclusions. The æsthetic sets everything in motion, starting a chain of activity that runs from reasoning to economic and ethic conduct. Without that perpetually renewed original act of 'æsthetic' the subsequent activities are either non-existent or they turn like the mill-stones that have no corn to grind. Thus arise the 'empty' abstractions of logic or intellectualism without æsthetic consent; economics in the abstract, ethics of a formal or husk-like character. And it is against these that both the real critic and the real prophet (indistinguishable in their philosophy) must and do inveigh, and both for the same reason, namely, that these activities are mimetic, mechanical, empty, being unrelated to the single source of reality which is æsthetic. Again, I will not quote Blake when all may read him; or only so much as pleases me: namely, this: 'If it were not for the Poetic or Prophetic Character, the Philosophical or Experimental would soon be at the Ratio of all things; and stand still, unable to do other than repeat the same dull round over again.' The terms are Blake's and can only be exactly understood by his readers; but the ideas are Croce's—or, shall we say simply, they are true? . . .

An American correspondent complains that *The New Age* is 'too inhuman in its abstract economics,' and this impression I know to be shared by some of our readers in England. But what would they have? It is true that in the actual world the most diverse things meet at some point and consequently appear to merge into one another; but the distinctions are only confounded but not obliterated by this. Grey is neither black nor white, but there still remain both black and white. Similarly economics and ethics remain distinct even when they are in some objects united. What our critics mean, perhaps, to say is that we not only separate in logic economics from ethics, but we argue as if this separation were inevitable in actual fact also. That, I do not doubt, is the substance of the charge against us; and I must repudiate it. For merely to recognize and insist (in the interests of clear thought, itself the precedent of good action) that economics and ethics are distinct and separable is not to affirm that they must or, still less, should remain unrelated. A right relation of ethics to economics can, in fact, be established only on the supposition that each is in its own fashion independent. Otherwise, one would be inseparable from the other, and economics would include ethics as ethics include economics. But this is not the case; and hence an autonomy (or Home Rule) must first be granted to economics, in order afterwards to have the right to demand its voluntary submission to ethics (which, on the analogy suggested, would be the inclusive yet autonomous Commonwealth). If, as I have continually to postulate, *The New Age* continues to afford us a platform for the full exposition of our ideas, our readers will be satisfied in time that our present insistence on the autonomy of economics is designed ultimately to make its subordinate co-operation with ethics easier. It is certainly our hope that one day the ethical conscience of our nation may be proud of its economic organization; but this virtuous pride is only possible when, first, the autonomy of economics is generally admitted, and, secondly, its recognition of the just dues of ethics is voluntarily offered. (*NA*, 14, 210, 1913.)

Are we to abandon every attempt to relate conscience with self-interest, or right with expediency? . . . Right, as I have heard it defined by one of the profoundest minds living, is might with long sight. In other words, as I venture to paraphrase it, virtue is immortal self-interest. . . .

In *Historical Materialism and the Economics of Karl Marx*, Benedetto Croce discusses the same problem, but in terms of economics and ethics. Marx, like his teacher, Hegel, was too apt to identify an abstraction made by the mind with the reality. He took economics, for instance, not only as a convenient point of view of life, but as a superior and deeper means of approach than any other. Economic materialism and the consequent economic interpretation of history were thus for him prime determinants; they explained everything. But Croce shows that other determinants are equally valid. Man is so mixed a creature that, in the end, it is impossible to limit his impulses and necessities to a single factor. Economics, it is true, is a determinant, but it is only one of many. Ethics is equally a necessity of life; and man can no more live without morality than without bread. Ethics, however, are not co-extensive with economics. Action may be economic without being ethical. On the other hand, ethical action must needs be economic, since the ethical is merely a selection of the economic. Applying this to the problem discussed by *The Times*, we may say that, though not all self-interest is moral, all moral acts are also self-interested. The 'moral' are a wise selection among acts which in themselves are non-moral. Morality is select economics. (*NA*, 15, 397, 1914.)

9 Economics: A Few Definitions (1917)

ECONOMICS—Is the science of production. The end proposed in economics is the production of the maximum amount of goods and services with the minimum expenditure of labour. To look at production with the eyes of the economist it is necessary to set aside human considerations, except in so far as they are assumed. . . . It is a mistake to suppose that because economics confines itself to the means of maximum production it is soulless. The soul of economics is politics, and it is to politics that economics relegates the control of questions such as what shall be produced, by whom, and how the results shall be distributed. There is presumably a perfect economic science in heaven; but it is ordered with perfect political art. On earth, economics is very imperfect; and politics is more imperfect still.

USE—Means in economics 'use towards making profit.' When Goldsmith's young Moses bought with good money of a pedlar some green spectacles that could not be used, he nevertheless purchased an economic commodity at the market-rate; which commodity had therefore an economic if not a human use. Capitalist production is production for use only incidentally. Its object is profit. The minimum of human use is often compatible with the maximum of economic use. A revolution in economics would be effected by exchanging a system of production for capitalist profit for a system of production for human use.

WAGE AND CHATTEL SLAVERY—An outcry was raised when somebody first called the proletariat wage-slaves and their condition one of wage-slavery. On the contrary, the wage-slaves profess to be free men, and regard their state as a great advance upon chattel-slavery or serfdom. But let us note that it was not by their exertions that the change from chatteldom to wagedom was brought about. If, therefore, it was progress for them, the motive was not theirs, nor do they deserve any credit for it. As for the advantages, let us see. In general, commercial men have discovered that for some forms of tool-labour hiring is cheaper than purchase. For instance, many printers prefer hiring their expensive type-setting machines to buying them outright. By this means, and for a comparatively small additional cost, they have the use of the machines without the real responsibility. Even amongst the old slave communities the axiom prevailed that it is cheaper to buy than to breed. This meant that it was less trouble and expense for a slave-owner to buy slaves already prepared for the market than to prepare them himself. A step further, and we are at the point in relation to men that printers are in relation to machines. The axiom, in short, of commercialism is that it is cheaper to hire labour than to own it. Why? For two reasons: In the first place, a man who owns labour and can hire no other is tied down to the skill his slaves happen to possess. He has not the free choice that an open market for labour gives him. And, in the second place, the privileges that were demanded by slaves grew to be excessive: they actually expected to be reared and educated, to have leisure while they were working, and provision made for illness and old age, as if they were human! The trouble alone was great, and the cost was terrible. How much better it would be to set the slaves at liberty and to throw upon themselves the burden of breeding, provision for sickness, and so on. Then the employers would have only their working years to consider. They could go into the proletariat quarters and select only the fit, leaving the unfit to die or to become fit at the expense of the rest. Is it not obvious from this consideration that if the substitution of wage-slavery for chattel-slavery, hiring for owning, was one step forward for labour, it was at least two for capital? And the proof is that capital has immensely increased its wealth, while the wages of labour are much the same as they were when labourers were chattels.

QUALITY AND QUANTITY—It is assumed that all commodities that make a market contain value or ability to satisfy human desire. What, then, is the economic distinction between Quality and Quantity? It is this: that Quality is concentrated satisfaction, while Quantity is diffused or diluted satisfaction. It will be observed that the element common to both is the ability to satisfy; and that the only difference between them is that qualitative goods satisfy intensely or for a long time, while quantitative goods satisfy only moderately or for a short time. But we know that the latter can in some cases be converted into the former: in other words, Quantity can be converted into Quality by the means of putting more work or labour into a commodity. Similarly Quality can be diluted into Quantity by skimping the work that is ordinarily put into it. This convertibility of the one into the other is the symbol of the convertibility of society into a better from being a worse, or into a worse from being a better. Commodities show the direction of the movement; and are, as it were, the index of the state of society. If, for example, we find that the majority of commodities in any given society are becoming qualitative in value, that is, contain more and more concentrated satisfaction, we know that society is itself becoming more qualitative in character, more value-producing, better organized, and therefore better. And if the reverse, then the worse. A tree is known by its fruit; Columbus knew the social condition of America by the wood-carvings he found adrift off its coasts; and a society is known by its commodities. Or the argument can be reversed. We can say that if a society becomes better organized, its products will tend away from Quantity—or diffused and unorganized value—and towards Quality—or organized value. It is not that society need be organized for qualitative production directly; for that is to subordinate human to economic values. It is simply that, as a consequence of a right ordering of society, economic values reach their maximum. Economics as a test of social virtue! Applying this to National Guilds, we may say that the object of National Guilds ought not to be the production of economic Quality, however necessary Quality is at this period in our history. The object of National Guilds, on the contrary, is economic justice. But as a consequence of economic justice, economic Quality will infallibly be produced. As the tree, so the fruit.

WEALTH—As the index of the prosperity of a hive of bees is the amount of honey the hive is capable of accumulating, economics looks upon society as a hive the measure of whose well-being is its wealth. Other sciences and philosophies measure the well-being of society by other standards: the happiness of the greatest number, numbers themselves, the state of religion, the state of art, etc. With these criteria economics has no quarrel; nor need they have any quarrel with economics. As an artistic or religious view of society must needs set up an artistic or religious standard: and neither is of necessity antagonistic to the other—that is to say, religion and art may well flourish together—so an economic view of society properly sets up for itself an economic standard with which, again, other standards are not necessarily inconsistent. An efficient economic society, that is to say, may be at the same time an artistic and a

10 Ethics, Economics, and Aesthetics (1916, 1918, 1912, 1915)

The æsthetic, as I have said before, is a trap for the unwary; and many are they who have fallen into it. . . . 'What [asks Clutton Brock in *A Modern Creed of Work*] is the real reason of the profound and growing discontent among our workers?' And he replies 'that they do not for the most part feel that their work is worth doing for its own sake,' but that it is 'producing rubbish without joy.' Does not the æsthete wish that it were so, and that the labour discontent could be shown to be an æsthetic revolt? But it is all a misconception and a misunderstanding to suppose it. The discontent, on the other hand, has it origins in regions both above and below the æsthetic plane. Below it is economic and personal, being a matter of wages and conditions; above it is ethical and personal, being a matter of justice and status. And neither of these is æsthetic, though both are susceptible of being inspired by a love which is not of the beautiful. The 'joy in work,' of which Mr. Clutton Brock writes as if it must needs refer to the work itself—æsthetic pleasure, in fact—is by no means necessarily absent even from the production of rubbish, or, still more astonishingly, from the production of something much worse than rubbish—witness the war, for example. It has usually, indeed, nothing to do with the 'thing' that is being produced, but everything to do with the spirit of the persons concerned, their sense of fellowship, their relations with their superiors, their *ethical* sense of the value and rightness of their occupation. If it were not so, it would be a poor look-out for work that cannot possibly in itself become æsthetic. (*NA*, 19, 446, 1916.)

It is not machinery but the wage system that is really at fault. To think otherwise, indeed, is . . . to fall into the materialist error of attributing spiritual effects to material causes. It is, moreover, to assume that technological processes are the parents instead of the products of economic phenomena. A free man—that is, one who is not exploited by a capitalist—cannot be 'enslaved' by a machine. He may, if he chooses, do nothing but machine-work all the days of his life, and still remain 'free.' The slavery and the degradation arise, not from the nature of the tools with which he works, but from the fact that under capitalism he himself is reduced to a tool. (*NA*, 22, 454, 1918.)

The literature and art of to-day are the parallels of the economic situation of to-day. A Socialist criticism of literature and art is, therefore, not impossible. That this criticism is necessary follows from the superior and prior relationship of art and literature to life. Materialists profess to be able to dispense with literature and art as *causes* of economic phenomena; but experiment proves that it is more easy to deduce economic phenomena from literary phenomena than vice versa. In other words, literature and art are more *significant* than economics and consequently more related to its causes than to its effects. Hence the necessity of literary and art criticism as at least a part of Socialist propaganda. What art and literature are to-day life will be to-morrow.

The proper reward of labour is the product of labour. Profit is adventitious and only came into existence with commercialism and the wage system. The aim of production for profit rapidly displaced the aim of production for intrinsic value; and so completely, that of all the commodities now made and sold for profit, only a small percentage possess any intrinsic value. Profiteering ruins good production.

The proper reward of art and literature is their product; and their product consists of (a) the pleasure, discipline and occupation of imagination and creation; and (b) the power thus obtained of satisfying, pleasing, or influencing others. This latter power may be exchanged for the material necessities of the artist's life.

Production for profit has displaced production for intrinsic values in art as in industry. As the capitalist exploits wage slaves primarily for profit, not primarily for production (being, in fact, anxious to increase profits at the expense of production: his motto: Maximum profits for minimum production), so the journalist exploits his literary and artistic gifts and reduces them to servile instruments of his profit. The journalist is, in the sphere of literature, both capitalist and wage slave.

The progressive decline of good production in manufacture is a direct consequence of profiteering. Similarly literature and art suffer progressive decline in intrinsic value with the rise of the literary profiteer. Nine out of ten books, pictures, plays, etc., exist only for the profit they produce; their intrinsic value is the minimum.

A blackleg in trade is one who sells his labour for less than his fellows can afford to sell theirs. There are blacklegs in literature who willingly forgo the proper rewards of literature, namely, its pleasure and the production of intrinsic value, in exchange for money profits. Literary profiteers are blackleg artists. But most blacklegs are also bad workmen.

Whoever writes for profit and not for use is either a wage slave or a capitalist. A willing wage slave is a potential capitalist. A capitalist is a promoted, but not emancipated, wage-slave. Every writer for profit, when he has acquired wealth, becomes a capitalist, or rather, proves himself to have been always a capitalist. Successful profiteering authors are shrewd investors.

The new Socialist critics of commercial art and literature are met by the same abuse as greeted the pioneers of Socialist criticism of economics. The literary world cannot be so bad, we are told. You are disgruntled fault-finders, critics with a personal grievance, wanton agitators on the make. And there are optimists and meliorists among readers of to-day as there are among political economists. These contend that the meanest book must contain something to praise and that improvement is constant. But would you praise the little wool in shoddy or the brown-paper in boot-soles? Can improvement result from the perpetual expansion of shoddy manufacture and the constant diminution of honest workmanship?

Few people realize—though it has been told them and proved to them—that most literary praise in the Press is paid for like the advertisements of patent medicines. A journal that depends on publishers' advertisements has no literary judgment. Its literary reviews and book notes are paid for by publishers and authors. In the interests of literature? No—in the interests of profiteering. ('Profiteering in Literature,' *NA*, 11, 232, 1912.)

The concluding paragraph of Señor Ramiro de Maeztu's article in last week's issue ought not to pass without our special attention. It links the literary mission of *The New Age* with the economic and the political. I have frequently commented on the fact that many of our readers appear to imagine that the subjects of economics and litera-ture, as treated in these columns, are separate in the minds of our writers as well as separable in fact. And as frequently I have assured them that they are wrong. The reason, I hope, has now been made clear; we are guildsmen in literary criticism, jealous *for* our profession, as we are guildsmen in economics, jealous *for* the welfare of industry. At present, it is plain, the judgment together with the reward of good literary workmanship is in the hands of the mob— from which it is as much our duty to deliver it as we have made it our duty to deliver the judgment and reward of industrial labour from the hands of profiteers. *Their* standard, like the standard of the mob in literature, is obviously not a craft standard; but refers to the profitability in commercial exchange of material products; as *this* refers to the mere capacity to tickle the ears of the groundlings. The popular author of to-day (there are at least a hundred making several thousand pounds a year) is very often the counterpart of the profiteer and, like him, exploits ignorance and other disabilities. We would have him judged and paid by his peers. (*NA*, 17, 13, 1915.)

11 Culture and Education (1911, 1918, 1915)

We have no right to expect that in a country like England of to-day, a large number of people will like anything really good. They would be a different people if they did.

Has not education made great strides?

Faugh! All we have done in education is to spread out, very thin, over many the culture that before was concentrated in a few. Everybody now has a scraping of culture, but there is no cultured class. That is what I complain of. Writers have watered down their art to the thickness of the veneer of culture in the largest class. They measure their work by its extension, and no longer by its intensity.

But you have surely no objection to this diffusion of culture.

None whatever,—on one condition, namely, that the supply of intense culture at the source is maintained. Against popular writers (shall we call them sophists?) I should have no grievance if they were not so inimical to pure literature. Unfortunately they are its bitterest enemies. . . . When Stevenson was alive, the most obscure young writer who showed promise was sure of a friendly letter. He and Henley between them 'fathered' half the young artists of their day. You see they felt communally and personally responsible. Knowing that the public could not discern good work at once, they employed their genius and position to discover and encourage it. Even Shaw quotes to-day with pride a letter which Stevenson wrote about him before he fell into popularity. What powerfully placed writer of to-day has taken Stevenson's great office of disinterested patronage? I know of none. But Stevenson had the instincts of an artist, and the sense of responsibility to his guild that our individualists have not.

Well, after all, it's a matter for writers. I do not see what the public has to do with it.

Not for the moment perhaps. There is still enough virtue in the diluted art provided by popular writers to satisfy the needs of the many. But I am looking a generation ahead. It is on the visions of dead artists that the world is living to-day; but what of the morrow if our living artists are now neglected? Our popular writers are killing the goose that lays the world's golden eggs. ('Unedited Opinions,' *NA*, 9, 35, 1911.)

The *Plymouth Co-operative News* publishes faithfully every month an analysis of the books issued to the people of Plymouth from the local free library. . . . Of 10,500 books issued during the month of March, 7,800 were classified as Fiction, 2,200 as Juvenile, and 260 as Magazines, leaving only some 250 of all the other kinds of books to a reading population of over 10,000. Fiction nowadays, we are told, is not what it used to be. We are told, indeed, that it is the modern university. It is certainly a very obliging medium. But on this very account it appears to me to be as delusive as it is obliging. It receives impressions easily, readily adapts itself to every kind of material, and assumes at the word of command any and every mood; but precisely because it does these things, the effects it produces are transient. Lightly come, lightly go; and if, as has been said, fiction is the modern reader's university, it is a school in which he learns everything and forgets everything. Modern as I am, and hopeful as I am of modernity, I cannot think that the predominance of fiction, even of such fiction as is written to-day, is a good sign; and when we see, in fact, that it leads nowhere, that the people who read much of it never read anything else, and that it is an intellectual cul-de-sac, our alarm at the phenomenon is the greater. What kind of minds do we expect to develop on a diet of forty parts fiction to two of all other forms of literature? Assuming the free libraries to be the continuation schools of the people, what is their value if the only lessons taken in them are the lessons of fiction? I will not dwell on the obvious discouragement the figures are to every serious *writer*; for the effect on the readers must be worse. (*NA*, 23, 27, 1918.)

It is very chivalrous of Professor Gide to enter the lists in our national defence against German criticism; but I do not know whether to thank him or not. In a recent issue of the *Daily News* he undertook to reply to Professor Sombart, who had written of us as follows:

A people of shopkeepers, incapable of any achievement of intellectual culture—either in the present or in the future—

whose philosophy, ethics, and religion are unadulterated manifestations of the spirit of the huckster . . . whose politics, like its morality, aims only at utility. It has only been able to create two things, comfort and sport; and these have contributed to destroy the last vestiges of its spiritual life.

But, in the first place, it is no defence to cite, as Professor Gide does, the great names of Newton, Milton and Shakespeare. These cannot be said to be achievements of our present. And, in the second place, we had better admit that there is some truth in the indictment. It is not, of course, altogether true; and to pronounce us incapable in the future of any intellectual achievement is to adopt the child of a mere German wish. But that we are for the moment and have been for twenty years incapable, as a nation, of maintaining, still less of transcending, our intellectual traditions is not alone a German discovery. Matthew Arnold announced it, and we have seen his forecast fulfilled. Let us confess our sins, the more certainly to amend our ways. . . .

It was not so long ago that I remarked in this column that other nations have some right to reproach us. Germany in particular. If Germany has never equalled our English culture at its best, Germany can yet maintain that, while she has been striving to do so, we have been falling away. After all, the question is one of fact in great part. If it can be shown that there are more people in Germany who understand and appreciate our *English* classics than there are in England itself, the verdict would be against us obviously. And I am afraid that either there are, or would soon have been. The majority of cultured Germans certainly know our Newton and our Shakespeare better than the majority of our own educated classes. As things were going, in a very little while I believe that most of our classics would have been comparatively neglected here as they became more and more familiar to Germany. If that is not a proper ground of reproach to us I do not know one. To fail even to understand, let alone to rival or surpass, our past achievements is surely almost a definition of decadence. And we were rapidly approaching that state. Unfortunately, too, the rot had gone so far that people were not even ashamed of it. We were all decadent together. Time was when for an educated man to have to confess ignorance of his national classics was a moral torture to be avoided by all diligence. Within the last ten years we have seen many leaders of literary opinion glory in the confession. If they, what shall mere readers be willing to confess? It is not surprising that they made a merit of absolving themselves from reading any classics whatever. Whether, as has been suggested, familiarity with our classics should be made obligatory on British citizens after the war I am not prepared to say; but only for the reason that I should not know how to enforce the regulation. Otherwise the same penalty should sanction the duty as now sanctions correct pronunciation and good manners, namely, ostracism from polite society. And the plea that no pleasure was taken in acquiring familiarity with the classics should not weigh with me either! No pleasure is taken for their own sake in exercises designed to make people healthy, beautiful, expert or polite—why should it be demanded of the exercises necessary to intelligence? Do you think the life, even of a professed student of literature and the arts, is all pleasure, and that never a disagreeable book *needs* to be read? (*NA*, 17, 382, 1915.)

Literature and Criticism

Many of Orage's statements concerning the nature of literature and criticism are likely to be accepted as true. That they do not appear to be original testifies to his reliance upon the English critical tradition and our general assent to principles that were seldom advocated in his time. Here we see the best exemplification of the 'brilliant common sense' that he attempted to attain in *The New Age* as a whole; in clarity and persuasiveness, several of the following passages are the equal of any that modern criticism has produced.

Those attentive to the theoretical consistency of criticism will note discrepancies in Orage's successive attempts to define literature between 1912 and 1922; they are discussed in the Introduction. His emphasis on criticism as a reason-giving activity and on critical judgment as ultimately dependent upon common assent remind one of Dr. Johnson and of recent æstheticians who have employed more sophisticated arguments to arrive at the same conclusions. His allusion to Jung in an argument against what he considered the misuse of Freudian theory in literary criticism, appearing in 1916, shows that he was acquainted with psycho-analysis and its limitations long before most of his contemporaries.

A literary column is not the most appropriate medium for the explication of poetry; when Orage undertook it, he was usually attempting to provide an object lesson for young poets whose work was appearing in little reviews. The best example of his practical criticism is a detailed comparison of passages from Shakespeare and Edward de Vere, intended to show that the latter was not a sufficiently skilful poet to have written Shakespeare's plays (*NA*, 28, 56 and 155–6, 1921).

12 On Reading (1916, 1915, 1912)

Why are we readers and writers? Assuming as an axiom the definition of man (there are few men yet!) as the truth-seeking creature, the further assumption must be made that since literature everywhere and always, by the acknowledged best minds of the race, is reckoned as honourable, literature in some way or other is a valuable instrument of truth. But in what way precisely? I have the disadvantage of being uncertain as to the facts of the following illustration, but it may nevertheless serve. They tell me that for the extraction of gold from quartz a new method, called the cyanide process, has been invented, by means of which the labour of the former method of crushing and washing has been considerably reduced. Be that as it may, in theory, at any rate, literature is a cyanide process applied to experience for the extraction therefrom of truth. Not all experience, as I have many times maintained, is of value to man as the truth-seeking creature: but only such experience as contains truth. And of this, again, there is, on the one hand, so little; and, on the other hand, the means of extracting truth from it are so difficult; that, without special good fortune or specially effective methods of extraction, a man may well live a dozen lives and yet learn little to his immortal advantage. It is the function of literature, therefore (or I conceive it to be), to communalize the particularly auriferous experiences of the fortunate (no man deserves to be called a literary man who is not, by nature, superlatively experiencing); and, at the same time, to demonstrate by example the most effective means of extracting truth from experience. Take any great book you please. Its two characteristics are, first, that it contains the record of the experiences of a rare and powerful mind; and, second, that it indicates in its method the means by which the writer turned his experiences to the account of truth. And we, the readers, by sympathetic following of him, are thus doubly instructed: in the first instance, by sharing in his experiences; and, in the second, by learning a means of turning our own to account. But is this not enough to establish the utility—yes, the utility—of literature,—utility being here defined as something that is useful to man as the truth-seeker? It is, I think—and yet there is much more to be said. But, perhaps, I have written enough. (*NA*, 18, 447, 1916.)

Quite a number of my readers have asked me to compile a list of the 'Best Hundred Books.' I was never enamoured of the idea and I am less so now than ever. What would in my opinion be of much greater value is the learning and appreciation of the 'Best Way to Read.' Read properly, fewer books than a hundred would suffice for a liberal education. Read superficially, the British Museum Library might still leave the student a barbarian. A book, after all, is no less difficult to understand than a man of the complexity of its author. Yet readers who would think ten summers and winters insufficient to enable them to pass judgment upon the personality of, say, Plato, will read his *Republic* once and be satisfied. But that is to have a nodding acquaintance, at best, with an author; and it compares with reading him as such as acquaintance compares with intimacy. To read in the sense worth speaking of is to live with a book for as long as one would need to live with the writer to become familiar with him. My own plan—if I may say so—is something of the kind. Necessary interruptions aside, I spend a week or so at a time with any writer worth my curiosity. I may not, after all, know many intimately; but such few as I do I know to the bone. (*NA*, 17, 477, 1915.)

Why are not literate people necessarily cultured, and cultured people necessarily literate? The distinction is not one of degree between culture and reading, but one of kind. There are two ways of reading: one is the literate and the other is the cultured way. And the difference between them is this: the merely literate person skims the meaning of what he reads and accepts or rejects it according to his first impression. He is an impressionist, trusting to the surface both of books and of his own mind for a report of what is. The cultured person, on the other hand, knows that both the written sentence and his own first impression are approximations only to truth. Each points, but neither does more than point. Thus in reading he inquires as well what the author says in words as what he meant to say, what he could have said, and what he failed to say. Sentence and lines for him are symbols of thought rather than complete expressions. They are thoughts in a certain stage of development, early and embryonic, or late and ripe, as the case may be. Culture divines the *age* of the sentence and the age of the thought behind it, also the nature of the mind in which it had its birth. But culture is similarly critical of itself—not sceptical, but waiting and attentive. Few deep impressions are instantly articulate. Few moods are self-conscious. Effects produced in the mind by books, etc., are almost never rightly estimated at the first trial, or if rightly not exactly. The habit of associating the good with the pleasant and the bad with the unpleasant is here a stumbling-block. What pleases one must needs be good; what displeases one must needs be bad. But here again culture suggests questions. Culture, we saw, divines in sentences their intention, their past and their future. Similarly, in the mood first induced by a book culture seeks to divine a past and a future. *Why* has this book immediately pleased me? Is the pleasure I feel due to its flattery of my weakness or to its nourishment of my strength? Again, is the pleasure I now feel likely to be permanent; will it last? Finally, if I were now called upon to act as I should desire to act, would the mood engendered by this book stimulate or depress me? All these questions both of the author and of himself the cultured reader asks and answers, at first consciously, but later unconsciously. But your literate person takes everything or nothing for granted. He is either a fanatic or a fool. Such readers are the terror of the cultured whether authors or readers themselves. ('On Reading,' *NA*, 11, 275, 1912.)

The difference between reading for pastime and reading to live accounts for the difference between dilettantism and criticism. For the former to read is an amusement, from which it is no odds whether he derives sustenance or wind. But for the latter to read is to feed, and upon his food depends in turn his own intellectual health. Guess, therefore, how at once real and personal such a reader becomes a critic; criticism is not for him a list of preferences but a table of necessities; it is his experience of the sustaining powers of books. I know myself that, in order to write a particular piece of work or to think out a difficult subject, I must read where strength is to be found. Swift, as I have often said, is in this respect meat and drink to me above all other writers. One essay of his—*The Conduct of the Allies*, say—and I feel in form for work and the equal of any of my contemporaries! Swift is perhaps a peculiarity of mine; all the eighteenth century writers are congenial to me; but I can live almost as well upon any of the great classics. They are classics *because* their substance is inexhaustible. (*NA*, 16, 695, 1915.)

13 The Nature of Literature (1915, 1914, 1913, 1922)

An anonymous writer in *The Nation* of last week gave me pleasure by coming very near my own definition of art, and then irritated me by retreating from it. A handful of us ought surely to be able to agree on the subject-matter of our profession; and most of all at a time like this, when the standards of criticism that will prevail after the war are being cast. Art, as I defined it (the idea is, of course, as old as the Himalayas!), is 'the imaginative perfecting of nature'; or the intuitive perception and representation of reality in actuality. *The Nation* goes the length of quoting Ben Jonson, who said of the art of poetry in particular: 'It utters somewhat above a mortal mouth'; and Poe, who said that 'it is no mere appreciation of the beauty before us, but a wild effort to reach the beauty above'; and even stretches out to Sidney's inspired oracle that nature's world 'is brazen, but the poets only deliver a golden'; and then, as I say, retreats in disorder. The oracle of Sidney, comments *The Nation*, is 'a fine saying rather than an interpretation . . . it has no importance as a theory of poetry to compare with Wordsworth's definition in the preface to his *Lyrical Ballads*.' On the contrary, as a description of the *spirit* of poetry, and of art in general, I find it infinitely to be preferred to Wordsworth's definition of the psychological method he, a single poet, employed. Sidney's sentence throws a light upon all poetry and all art, Wordsworth's upon—Wordsworth! (*NA*, 17, 13, 1915.)

There are two kinds of realism: that which works after nature, and that which works in the spirit of nature; and it is the first form alone which I believe and hope to be dead. The second, on the contrary, is always living, though sometimes less and sometimes more. My hope is to see this kind of realism flourish as the other moulders.

This true realism, or creation in the spirit of nature, is again two-formed. One kind divines the potential reality, and the other divines the intention. We may say, I think, that prolific and multifarious as nature is, her course is still only one among a thousand possible. Of all the routes by which man has been reached, was the actual route taken the only conceivable? There may have been—and possibly there were—many other routes begun and abandoned before the route actual was finally determined. The first form of imaginative realism has its sphere here: it divines what nature could and she would: what, in fact, might have been or still may be (for life is not over yet). And the second form has its sphere in the world of the actual becoming. What nature not only *can*, but has a mind to— this is the material of the realism of the second order.

The pitch is high, but by no means too high for the dignity of literature. Nothing is more depressing to a critic than to witness the ease with which writers of no creative ability whatever reach by acclamation a 'front rank.' They have only to copy nature slavishly to be greeted as creative artists. Why, to copy nature is one of the easiest things in the world. At least ten thousand reporters do it daily. From the front are pouring every day 'realist' descriptions of battle which no professional 'realist' writer could equal. Tolstoy, Zola, Stephen Crane, all appear to me to be absolutely beaten at their own game by any casual soldier writing home to a sympathetic friend. If a description of what is, of so-called actuality, be the final aim of literature we ought to flatter ourselves that pretty well anybody can reach it. There is nothing, then, in the literary profession to brag about or to call for special respect. Our novelists only differ from our rank and file by reason of their greater leisure and lesser experiences. Literature, in short, is reduced to nothing of importance.

The true realism, on the other hand, raises literature to a great art again. No mere record of experience, however novel, here obtains an entrance. Admission is by divination not by description. Compare, for instance, the descriptions of battles in Homer and in the *Mahabharata* with the descriptions of actuality. The latter are accurate, but the former are true. There never was such a battle as Vyasa described in the *Mahabharata*. There probably never will be. But, as we read it, we feel that nature has dreamed it, and only *not* actualized it because she had other plans. By this means, actuality itself becomes transfigured; experience is given a solace; and no mere reporting can accomplish that. What is the satisfaction in knowing that such and such a thing occurred? But there is a satisfaction in knowing that it occurred as a consequence of a choice among many alternatives! Freedom is given back to us. At each moment we stand at a new cross-roads. The road nature takes will be, in course of time, the actual; the roads she passes will remain the potential. The more of all of them there are the richer life has become for us.

I recall Coleridge's remarks on Deborah's Song. 'When I read the Song of Deborah,' he said, 'I never think that she is a poet, although I think the song itself a sublime poem.' Why is this remark just? The answer is to be found in the remark of Aristotle that 'of all works of art, those are the most excellent wherein chance has the least to do.' But for the chance of her exploit, Deborah would have remained dumb. But for the chance of their experiences most of our soldiers at the front would never have written a line of literature. But for the chance of this or that, the material of our novelists would never have fallen their way. They are as dependent upon chance as any reporter sent out of a morning to pick up a 'story.' There is no art in it, no creation; it is simply luck.

That, in spite of the multitude of creative artists among us, there is no creation is evident from this fact: that, outside a few figures (Sherlock Holmes is the most notable) not a character in modern fiction has leapt out of its book. Dickens, on the other hand, seems to have been a veritable master in nature's workshop. He seems to have watched nature at work, to have acquired her trick, and to have bettered her instruction. The London of his day certainly afforded nature an opportunity for ingenious creation; but even life was not more inventive than Dickens. At the same time he is vastly inferior to Shakespeare and the major artists. It is true he worked in the spirit of nature, but as her assistant, not as her prophet and seer. What nature could do and was already doing, Dickens could do as well as she. But what nature was still striving to do, and as yet could not actualize, Shakespeare did in imagination in advance of her. Shakespeare, in short, created more easily than nature, while Dickens created only *as* easily as nature. Look at Falstaff, for example. What approximations to him nature has made and, let us hope, is still making. There was no holding up the mirror to nature when Shakespeare created Falstaff. Rather it was the holding up of a telescope to nature! Now Dickens never held up a mirror (as our 'realists' do); nor did he hold up a telescope; but his mind was a kaleidoscope. (*NA*, 16, 538–9, 1915.)

What is reality for the purposes of art? *Not* actuality, for otherwise art would be simply reproductive. Then what? I take it that the reality with which art deals is the potentially actual—not what is, but what might be. Its world thus has the same laws as ours, but a different succession of events and a different convention. True comedy, for instance, is a variant of life as we know it; its materials are ours but the standards of value in it are different. When the Restoration comedists figured a society in which fidelity, truthfulness, and honour simply did not exist, they employed, it is true, as lay figures, the people around them, but with no intention, I firmly believe, of bringing these standards into disrepute. On the contrary, by exhibiting a world of manners from which these qualities were absent, and exhibiting it in its best and gayest light, they appear to me to have done so in the certainty that, even so, such a world was inferior to the actual. I may be wrong in this; but the apologies of Dryden, Congreve and Wycherley certainly bear me out. Each wrote comedies of an immoral world (that is, of a world with different morals from our own), but each took as much care to praise the morals of this as to describe the morals of that. After all, is not that what the complete artist would do, accept in the practical world the morals of the practical world; and in the imagined world the appropriately imagined morals? . . .

I myself would claim quite loudly that all great art is propagandist: only I should then ask what the propaganda is and what are the methods peculiar to the dramatic art; for it is upon these that everything turns. To my mind the propaganda of art is truth—truth actual or truth potential: in a phrase, art attempts to reveal the spiritual structure of the world with which it deals. (*NA*, 15, 157, 1914.)

[Concerning Richard Curle's *Joseph Conrad: A Study*, 1914:] Far from 'wrecking,' as Mr. Curle says, 'the meaning of a work of art' by examining it philosophically, if it cannot stand that, it cannot stand time. And Conrad, moreover, has nothing to fear from such an examination. On the contrary, our appreciation of his work will grow as we plumb his mind and try its depths. . . . I am not sure that the 'futility of the world' properly describes an article of Mr. Conrad's creed; I am pretty sure, in fact, that it does not; for the world, I imagine, exists for Mr. Conrad *to be understood*. (*NA*, 15, 181, 1914.)

In *The English Review* for July Mr. Henry Newbolt delivers himself

of some fallacious remarks on the value of criticism. . . . Mr.
Newbolt is under the popular superstition that a work of art or of
criticism depends for its value upon its success in 'expressing the
feeling of the writer and communicating it to those who read.'
Tolstoy it was who started that March hare. The value of a work of
art lies in its expression of truth. Its author is of no more concern to
us than is the creator of flowers when we look upon and enjoy their
beauty. We may, if we choose, be led to wonder what manner of
intelligence created them; we may even in imagination rise to
reverence and love. But these are secondary phenomena in the strict
sense. The flowers or the works of art are equally beautiful whether
we seek to divine through them a personal creator or not. Similarly I
am certain that artists hate the phrases 'self-expression' and
'communication'; the ideas are repulsive and quite incompatible
with an artistic impulse, the essence of which is spontaneity,
apparent causelessness, apparent purposelessness. Mr. Newbolt
goes even further astray when he declares *Paradise Lost* to be not
one of the world's great epics, on the ground that its theology is
antiquated. We do not, he says, now number Adam and Eve among
our ancestors. But who are 'we'? As a 'myth' the story of Adam and
Eve contains, as Johnson said, the substance of truth. It is not, of
course, scientific description; but it is precisely and exactly artistic
representation; and I do not know at this moment any more accurate
artistic hypothesis for the facts of human life than the story of
Genesis. Not on the ground of its 'antiquated' theory, therefore, is
Milton's epic dismissible. Nor on any other ground. As long as
mountains are impressive (needing no periodical readjustment of
critical values), or the sea and the sky inspire men with awe and
wonder, Milton's verse will retain its power, for it is one with them.
(*NA*, 13, 297, 1913.)

We may agree with Croce that all art is expression without agreeing
with him that all expression is art. *Qua* expression, expression is—
expression; and a quite different concept must enter before we can
convert the equation into 'expression is art.' Nor is the matter
settled by attempting to discover which expressions are art and
which are not, since the 'art' of the expression is not so much in the
expression as in the effect produced. Putting it another way, we
can say, however, that those expressions, and only those, are 'artistic'
that produce the effect of art by deliberate designs. But what is this
'effect of art'? It is sometimes imagined that an artistic effect is one

that is 'felt'; in other words, it is said to be an emotion of some kind. In this case, the success of a 'work of art' is assumed to lie in the transfer of the emotion of the artist to the experience of the beholder; and the latter is said to 'appreciate' the work because he has been made to re-produce the emotions of the artist who created it. Or, again, it is sometimes assumed that a work of art is successful in proportion to the number and quality of the 'ideas' it stimulates in the spectator or hearer or reader. A given quantity of ideas or a given quality of ideas, when it reaches a certain degree of intensity, is said to be the result of art and to entitle the canvas or sonata or essay to be regarded as a work of art. Here, too, the success is assumed to be due to the transfer of the artist's ideas to his beholder, hearer or reader. Considerable difficulties arise from accepting either of these theories or any combination or modification of them. For instance, it is well known that artists sometimes 'convey' much more emotion and many more ideas than they themselves have ever experienced. This is particularly true of musicians and painters. Again, the theory assumes that the artist is in a high degree of emotion when expressing himself or that he is, as we say, 'full of ideas'—states of mind which, however desirable in themselves, are certainly not conducive to the production of a work of art. As regards the beholder, the same difficulties arise. Must he call a work of art the piece that has 'moved' him; or the piece that has stirred the greatest number of ideas in him? But in that case, very low forms of art and, often, no art at all must be given the credit; for we have all felt considerable emotion and experienced many ideas from subjects which by common consent are not in the category of art at all. The conclusion to be drawn is the somewhat startling one, that art has nothing to do either with emotions or with ideas. Neither feeling nor intellect, in the precise sense, is engaged either in the production or in the appreciation of a work of art; but some power of the mind to which it is difficult to give an exact name. Let us suppose, however, that, in the main, emotions derive from the subconscious, and 'ideas' from the conscious. Art, having to do with neither, can then be assumed to be the medium for the expression of the superconscious, the characteristic activity of which we may call contemplation. With this classification, the nature and purpose of art become not only intelligible, but simple. Art arises from the creative contemplation of the artist and arouses in the beholders a corresponding appreciative contemplation. Both artist and critic are on the superconscious plane; the one creating symbols for its expression and the other experiencing its life in contemplation. All art thus plunges the beholder into a high state of reverie or wonder or contemplation or meditation; and that is both its nature and its purpose. We should suspect a work professing to be art when it arouses either caution or thought. Unless it can still both of these inferior states, and arouse us to contemplation, it is human, all too human. ('A Reformer's Note-Book: Art,' *NA*, 31, 300, 1922.)

14 Critical Judgment (1920, 1918, 1913, 1914)

It is a good plan, when one has finished reading a book, to sit down and ask oneself not only 'What do I think of this book?' but 'What shall I always think of it?' The courts of appeal and judgment in the mind are many, and they range from courts of first instance, where a rough and ready sort of opinion is given, to the final court, where final judgments are dispensed; in other words, those judgments which are the individual's very own and which he cannot change without changing himself. For minor literary offences, petty larcenies and the like, the court of first instance is sufficiently just. To trouble the higher court to deliver considered judgment on the mass of published literature would be to be guilty of vexatious and frivolous litigation. It is almost a matter of indifference what one thinks about, let us say, the novels of Mr. W. J. Locke or Miss Marie Corelli—and the list might be extended indefinitely to cover much more respectable names. Judgment au fond about such writers is much the same thing as judgment at a glance; nothing valuable is lost by it. On the other hand, there are books and writers who demand to be brought before the highest court of one's consciousness and for whom a judgment au fond, from the bottom of one's soul, is an obligation of every kind of honour. The effort required to bring them there is, I know, considerable; and even greater is the mental effort required to pass a final judgment that will last the whole of one's life on them. Nevertheless, they deserve it; and if we ourselves have it in us, they provoke it. The mind cannot rest until it has done them justice. (*NA*, 27, 7, 1920.)

This raises the old question whether criticism—art criticism in general—is or can be anything more than an expression of personal preference; whether its whole character, in fact, is idiosyncratic; and in the most recent issue of a very meritorious little art quarterly, *Root and Branch*, I find it being debated by the editor, Mr. James

Guthrie. Mr. Guthrie's opinion is not in the least uncertain; he has no doubt about it. Not only, he says, is a universal or final judgment of a work of art impossible, but we artists do not require it of any critic. . . . What is interesting is the mentality that lies behind the critic's expression of opinion. Nothing, it appears to me, can be more wrong and even self-contradictory than such an attitude. To abandon the aim of 'finality' of judgment is to let in the jungle into the cultivated world of art; it is to invite Tom, Dick and Harry to offer their opinions as of equal value with the opinions of the cultivated. Moreover, it is no escape from this conclusion to inquire into the 'mentality' of the critic and to attach importance to his judgment, as his mentality is or is not interesting. I am not in the least concerned in appraising a judgment with the mentality, interesting or otherwise, of the judge who delivers it. My concern, in fact, is not with him, but with the work before us; nor is the remark I am looking forward to making upon his verdict the personal comment: 'How interesting!' but the critical comment, rather, of 'How true!' Personal preferences, such as Mr. Guthrie desiderates, turn the attention in the nature of the case from the object criticised to the person criticising. The method substitutes for the criticism of art, the criticism of psychology. In a word, it is not art criticism at all.

But it will be said that if we dismiss personal preference as a criticism of art judgment, there is either nothing left or only some 'scientific' standard which, again, has no relevance to æsthetics. This, in fact, is the common plea of the idiosyncrats, that, inconclusive as their opinions must be, and anything but universally valid, no other method within the world of art is possible. I emphatically dissent. I am of opinion that a 'final' judgment is as possible of a work of art as of any other manifestation of the spirit of man; and that there is nothing in the nature of things to prevent men arriving at a universally valid (that is, universally accepted) judgment of a book, a picture, a sonata, a statue or a building any more than there is to prevent a legal judge from arriving at a right judgment concerning any other human act. And, what is more, such judgments of art are not only daily made, but in the end they actually prevail and constitute in their totality the tradition of art. The test, however, I am willing to agree, is not scientific; but as little, I protest, is it merely personal. Its essential character, in fact, is simply that it is right; right however arrived at, and right whoever arrives at it. That the judge in question may or may not have 'studied' the history of the art-work he is judging is a matter of indifference. Neither his learning nor his natural ignorance is of any importance. That, again, he is or is not notoriously this or that or the other is likewise no concern of mine. All that matters is that his judgment, when delivered, should be 'right.' But who is to settle this, it may be asked? Who is to confirm a right judgment or to dispute a wrong one? The answer is contained in the true interpretation of the mis-understood saying: De gustibus non est disputandum. The proof of right taste is that there is no real dispute about its judgment; its finality is evidenced by the cessation of debate. Or, as it may be simply stated, a judge—that is to say, a true judge—is he with whom everybody is compelled to agree, not because he says it, but because it is so. (*NA*, 24, 25-6, 1918.)

My most general opinion, perhaps, of the condition of modern English literature is this: that as good writers exist potentially to-day as at any time, save the greatest in our history; but that our critics are, without exaggeration, the worst ever known in any world of letters. I do *not* complain, let it be noted, that our critics do not praise enough; they praise far too much. Praise is so cheap to-day that any fool can buy it by the column in almost any journal. Nor do I complain that there is not blame enough distributed by the critics of the press. Up and down there is plenty of it. The real charge to be brought against the dispensers of censure and en-comium is that they distribute these precious wares with no respect for the established laws of literature; in short, their criticism is ignorant. Now, say that you like about the stimulus of praise, its value to a sincere writer is nil when he knows that its author simply pours it out by the bucketful. And the same applies to blame when it is distributed by no discernible principle. What I should like to see is reasons given for every judgment. When the judge delivers sentence it should be after a summing-up on the evidence actually before both court and jury; and his principles of judgment should be the established principles of the world's literature. This may seem a Utopian demand, but actually it is no more difficult in the case of literature than in the case of law. To many of the law's best judgments very few juries could come by their own accord, and certainly never by the way taken by the judges themselves; never-theless, when delivered and with evidence accompanying them, these best judgments commend themselves to the common sense even of the average jury. Similarly, I believe, any average body of readers could be brought to appreciate the justness of every sound literary judgment, provided they could be induced to follow the evidence. The unjustness of certain judgments likewise might as easily be brought home to them. I appeal for a more careful reading and for a more careful judgment in literary matters. Above all, I appeal for evidence in every case, and for such evidence as an honest though plain man cannot reject. (*NA*, 13, 761, 1913.)

In *The Times Literary Supplement* of May 14, Mrs. Wharton continues the discussion opened recently by Mr. Henry James on the subject of the criticism of fiction. Mr. James, it may be recalled, said bluntly what I have often said obliquely, namely, that in England there is no longer any such thing as literary criticism. Mrs. Wharton regrets the fact and proceeds to give first aid to critics—particularly critics of novels. They should, she says, ask three questions concerning a work of art: what has the author tried to represent; has he succeeded; and was the subject worth representing? But the value of these three is, to my mind, conditioned by the answer to a fourth question: what is the purpose of representation at all? Plainly representation in itself is not sufficient to create a work of art, since, ex hypothesi, some things are and some things are not 'worth representing.' What are the things worth representing and why are they worth it? This reduces itself to a question of values; and this, again, to a philosophy of life. Hence it follows that no novelist who is without a philosophy of life is or can be an artist. But equally with the artist the critic needs his table of values by means of which to estimate the works of representation; in other words, he, too, needs a philosophy. And this is just where both classes at present are at a loss; for we may say that there *is* no philosophy to-day. Thus it comes about that few novels are worth reading and still fewer are worth reviewing. Our critics, I may say, have long given it up as a waste of time. (*NA*, 15, 62, 1914.)

15 The Function of Criticism (1914, 1916, 1913)

Lessing's *Laokoon*, which I have just been re-reading in the shilling Bohn edition is a fine example of German criticism in the period before the Fall. Of Lessing Goethe said that 'his lot was to live in such a wretched age that his life was one long polemical effort.' But why should it not have been? Every age requires its contemporary, even more than it requires its succeeding critic; and it is a poor age that cannot spare an artist for the purpose or inspire one to the perilous thankless duty. Lessing, it is true, might have been a dramatist had he not chosen the office of critic; but his immediate successors would have found their path more thorny in consequence. Goethe, I believe, owed a part of his serenity to the peace the polemical Lessing created for German culture. Matthew Arnold—with, however, a little more fastidiousness—drudged at much the same task in England. He, too, might have been—nay, he was—a poet; but preferred the more public-spirited office of scape-goat-censor. Let nobody blame him—except that he left so many dragons still alive! Lessing's *Laokoon*, like Arnold's *On Translating Homer*, is not ephemeral criticism either. It is a polemic for all time. Goethe read it with enthusiasm as a student at Leipsic and with the same enthusiasm as a brahman preceptor at Weimar. Herder read it through three times in a single afternoon and evening (that's the way to read!), and our own Macaulay, the accomplished Philistine, told Lewes that he had learned more taste from it than from any other book. That, I think, is not to be in need of Goethe's apology! Lessing needs no excuse. (*NA*, 16, 197, 1914.)

With the exception of Russia, every European country with a literature possesses at the same time a highly developed criticism. The latter may not be popularly supposed to be the condition of the former; and, perhaps, if I nevertheless maintain it, the case of Russia may be cited against me. But Russia is the exception that proves the rule. Practically there are no good *little* writers in Russia: they are all either mediocre or great. But why not? Criticism does not create literature—but it prepares appreciation for it, and, above all, it extends the domain of the good. Criticism is to literature what a reader is to a writer. Hence, by the way, the folly of our publishers in insisting upon praise instead of upon criticism. By denying the general reader the education that comes of criticism they are preparing for themselves a public that in the end will read only tenth-rate works; and thus public and publishers will be deeper and deeper in the mire. Russia—to return to my subject—had the makings of a great critic in Volinsky, who is still alive, though now an old man. Thirty years ago he began a critical series of Russian literary studies that promised to endow Russia with the equivalent of the French S.-Beuve. But he was too much for the chauvinists; he was unpatriotic enough to find faults to condemn as well as excellences to praise. And they managed to silence him. Since then, I believe, he has written nothing; though he has thought a great deal. (*NA*, 18, 372, 1916.)

The claim of Mr. Eden Phillpotts to speak for 'us artists' is sufficiently impudent without his further claim for artists to be above ethical criticism. Writing in *The Times* in reply to the Headmaster of Eton he asks whether the artistic 'specialist' is alone to be at the mercy of the world, of the same world that 'stands in respectful silence before the technical operations of a plumber.' The artist, he says, 'is in the world to give the world what it cannot possess without him,' for 'he who merely offers what his neighbour's dim eyes can perceive for themselves has no excuse for his artistic existence.' I will not make the obvious retort on Mr. Phillpotts; but will reply that unless the artist shows us truth we do not want to see his work, and of truth 'us critics' have as good an idea as any artist that ever lived. Boast for boast, in fact, we have a better idea of truth than artists; for while they produce for our appreciation it is we who by still a subsequent act judge. I am quite prepared, of course, to admit that judges are few; but I am not prepared to admit that artists can distinguish them. The artist demands praise and praise only; the judge ignores his demand, or, rather, satisfies it, but in his own way which is criticism: a way the artist usually fails to approve! Assuming for the sake of argument that Mr. Phillpotts is the typical artist, can he truthfully say that had the Headmaster of Eton praised his works, he would have resented

---

Being in most cases irresponsible by necessity, reviewers were
bound sooner or later to make a virtue of it. In *The Times* review of
Mr. Wells' *The Passionate Friends* . . . the writer remarks: 'It is not
the business of the reviewer to pass moral judgments on the persons
of the novel.' His sole business, apparently, is to say whether the
characters are plausible and consistent. But this paltry unmoral
attitude is not only a cowardly retreat from the duties of criticism, it
is impossible consistently to mortal man. In this same review, for
example, the writer concludes that there is no lesson to be taken
from the fate of Lady Mary. What is this, if not a moral judgment—
of a kind, at least? Like literature in general, the good critic takes
all life for his province. More even than other writers, his business is
to find the truth about things and to propagate it. I can conceive an
artist writing with no propaganda in mind—though such are rare if
not altogether non-existent—but I can imagine no critic worth his
office who does not judge with a single eye to the upholding of the
moral laws. Far from being an offence to literature, this attitude of
the true critic does literature honour. It assumes that literature
affects life for better or worse. (*NA*, 13, 634, 1913.)

In another part of the present issue appears, I am told, a letter
from Mr. R. B. Kerr in which he charges me with showing a strong
tendency to subject the æsthetic to the ethical in my criticisms of
literature. Really I do not think that such a charge can be truthfully
said to lie against me; and Mr. Kerr, I note, offers no examples,
though I have been writing encyclopædically for a hundred or more
weeks. The accusation nevertheless irks me a little, for I see that I
must have given so fair a critic an excuse for it. Let me then explain
myself. The first ground that could conceivably be taken against me
is that I subordinate my valuation of a man's work to my valuation of
his personal character—after the manner of the Puritans, who deny

that good can come out of Galilee. But the very reverse of this is actually my case, for I contend that a man's character is revealed in his work as it is not and cannot be in his mere life. ('As for living,' said Villiers de l'Isle Adam for every artist, 'our servants can do that for us.') Do not tell me, I have often said to biographers, what porridge had John Keats or what earthly experiences befell Shelley. Only in so far as these things show in style are they of any possible value; and, without knowing them at all, the critic can divine as much of them as he needs. The style is the man; and his works are his life—all his life, at least, that concerns the literary critic. Next it might be assumed that I import moral decadence as exhibited in personal character into literature and find there what I presumably look for. But it is not so. Any moral decadence, so-called, that conceals itself from the eye of the critic of pure literature is to my mind irrelevant to criticism. Either it is discoverable in the style or it is not; and if not, what have I, as a critic, to do with it? I do, however, contend, that moral decadence may be discovered in style itself. It is shown, as I have often observed, in the very construction of a man's sentences, in his rhythm, in his syntax. That a man who writes badly has the seeds of bad conduct in him I firmly believe; but, qua critic, it is his bad writing I complain of, and not its after or before effects in his conduct. Lastly, I imagine it may be held that my condemnation of certain writers' choice of subject is itself proof of a moral bias in æsthetic matters. But, here again, my criterion is purely literary. Theoretically, every subject is open to every writer; but practically every writer chooses the subject that best suits his powers. Because there is admittedly a hierarchy of subjects —for Mr. Kerr will not contend that the subject of *Paradise Lost* is not grander than the subject of Swinburne's 'Dolores'—must I not place in the front rank the writers whose choice of subject is elevated and who write up to it; and in a lower rank the writers who choose petty subjects even when they write up to these? And the consciousness of power that impels a man to the former choice is evidence at the same time of his wholeness; as the consciousness of only a little power that leads to the lower choice is also evidence of a writer's failure in wholeness—in short, of his decadence. Decadence, as Mr. Kerr suggests, is at once a moral and an æsthetic term; but my defence is that in these notes I have never used it unwittingly in the former sense. Decadence, for me as a critic, is absence of a mission, of a purpose, of a co-ordination of powers; and its sign manual in style is the diffuse sentence, the partial treatment, the inchoate vocabulary, the mixed principles. When I have discovered these I would, it is true, hand the writer over to a critic to be cured—but only of bad style of mind. Ministering to a style diseased is one of the peculiar tasks of the critic. (*NA*, 18, 85, 1915.)

To endeavour to penetrate Hamlet's mystery further than Shakespeare penetrated it himself is to go outside the boundaries of art into the region of science. It is to be not Hamlet's critic, but his medical attendant. . . . Without denying, for a moment, the possible medical and psychological discoveries possible upon these lines, what I am concerned to point out is their irrelevance to literary or artistic criticism. Art is not concerned with origins, but with outcomes. To use Jung's illustration (to which 'A. E. R.' takes objection), art is not concerned with the mineralogical elements of Cologne Cathedral, but with the form and design of the cathedral itself. . . . Psychoanalysis, I agree with 'A. E. R.,' has come to stay. All I suggest is that it should stay where it belongs. As a means to the study of psychology, it is invaluable; it has about as much to do with art and literature as stethoscopic observation has to do with love lyrics of English poetry. One is science, the other is art. (*NA*, 19, 134, 1916.)

Hamlet . . . may have suffered from suppressed incestuous desires, and the suppression coupled with the failure to discover and to confess to himself their nature may have resulted in the inhibition of which his will in particular directions was the victim. All this, I say, may be true, and probably is true; and in this event the play of Hamlet is a dream of Shakespeare, of which the key has been found by psycho-analysts. My objection, however, to this interpretation or diagnosis was the purely literary objection of irrelevance to literary criticism. Literary criticism, I maintain, penetrates no further than literature on peril of being transformed into another kind of criticism altogether. Exactly as on passing from the appreciation of a pearl as a pearl to the examination of a pearl as the disease of an oyster we pass from æsthetics to biology, so in psycho-analysing the mood of Hamlet we pass from literature to therapeutics. That was my attitude then; and it is my attitude now when I understand a good deal more of psycho-analysis than I did a few years ago. (*NA*, 22, 271, 1918.)

17 Judging Contemporary Literature (1920, 1914)

The late Sir E. T. Cook's *More Literary Recreations* contains a great deal of pleasant gossip about books and bookmen, but none of it is strikingly original. . . . He seldom ventured it upon anything that had not become well established; and when he did it was to declare that two lines like the following had 'the poignancy of true poetry':—

> When dreamless rest is mine, I shall not need
> The tenderness for which I long to-night.

That, of course, is sentiment, and mawkish sentiment at that. It is not poignant, it is not true, and it is not poetry.

Without being too harsh, it is still possible to wish that men of the stamp of the late Sir E. T. Cook, and including the majority of our literary professors, could be brought to the test more frequently. While they drone away on the 'classics' they can seldom be convicted of positive lack of taste; but, presented with new work without a previous 'safe' judgment to steer by, they would, I am quite certain, usually come to grief. Sir E. T. Cook, as I have just remarked, pronounced the poem from which two lines have been quoted to be 'true poetry.' That finishes him. But how many of our present-day professors would survive the same test? Put before them the new work of some anonymous writer and ask them to 'place' it—how many would succeed in appreciating it? They usually know their limitations, however, and avoid the trap. Almost the definition of a professor of literature is that he passes judgment only on the dead or the successful! (*NA*, 26, 207, 1920.)

It has just occurred to me why I so often hate to read the eulogies of the dead. This Mr. Watt now—with his rhetoric about the dead Burns and his throbbing this and flaming that—what would he make of Burns alive yet obscure? Probably nothing; and his case is common. Critics feel it *safe* to write about the dead, for nobody cares to correct them. Besides, they need only to read a dozen or so essays about a dead man to come without effort to an apparent judgment of their own. In the case of the living, however, they both risk a little, and are compelled to be original; and hence usually their failure. On the whole I prefer the criticisms written during an author's life to any written afterwards. So, I believe, do authors. (*NA*, 14, 499, 1914.)

18 Practical Criticism (1917, 1914, 1920)

Stevenson had a false modesty upon the subject of literary analysis which did his admirable curiosity no honour. Even while he was engaged in it, and enjoying the exercise thoroughly, he pretended to feel like a vandal pulling a rose to pieces to discover the secret of its beauty. The exercise is, however, comparable to nothing of the kind, nor is it even comparable to another analysis to which Stevenson likened it, that of a child pulling a musical-box to pieces. In these cases, as you will observe, the rose and the box are destroyed in the process; but in the former case the wonder and the beauty of literature remain, and are, in fact, enhanced in our realization of them by the very process of analysis, or pulling literature to pieces. If it were, indeed, the case that after a careful analysis a poem or an essay ceased to be beautiful for us, richly would our analysis have rewarded us; for the refinement of our sense of beauty is essential to the appreciation of excelling work. But upon many occasions in English literature—praise be to famous men—the more you analyse it the more mysteriously beautiful it becomes. The process is then rather like anatomizing the body in fear of destroying the soul, but only to discover that the soul is thereby isolated beyond us. As all that can be anatomized is precisely not life, so all that can really be analysed is precisely not literature; for literature stands to writing as life stands to body. Let us analyse away, then, as hard as we please, and with a good conscience. We shall discover many secrets by its means, but we shall never destroy but only isolate the mystery of literature. (*NA*, 21, 267, 1917.)

To *The Nation*, and in an article almost next door to 'Penguin's' lament for the collapse of literary criticism, Mr. Bridges is the 'supremely cultured poet,' and almost everything he writes is a marvel. 'No poet,' you will be thrilled to hear, 'has derived more from the open air'—no, not the open-air *cure*, but simply the open air. His poetry thrives upon it. Consider only the 'rare beauty of these lines,' for instance, all derived obviously from the open air, and 'perfectly marrying sound and imagery.' Consider:

> The Lenten lilies, through the frost that push,
>   Their yellow heads withhold:
> The woodland willow stands a lonely bush
>   Of nebulous gold;
> There the spring goddess cowers in faint attire
>   Of frightened fire.

Before daring to form an opinion of this perfect marriage listen to *The Nation*'s epithalamium: 'Only the finest mastery of technique could have captured in mid-flight that subtle vision of beauty without any apparent effort and without shaking the bloom on its wings.' Now it is our turn!

No 'apparent effort' in the two inversions that make the first two lines; no 'apparent effort' in creating a *lonely* bush out of a *woodland* willow; no 'apparent effort' in duplicating the idea of timidity in 'cowers' and 'frightened'; no 'apparent effort' in chiming the fourth and sixth lines; no 'apparent effort' in the four alliterative pairs of words! Why, the effort is not only apparent, but it is unsuccessful. The first two lines convey to me no image whatever; the second two carry a commonplace picture; and the third pair conveys the most unfitting image of the goddess in the attitude of humiliation. And what is the whole intended to present or suggest? I declare that it is not even a whole. The 'bush' may pass as suggesting the goddess; but where is the 'there' where she cowers, and what have the lilies to do with the place? Well, well, that's enough! Besides, it seems that such remarks are out of order. *The Nation* says: 'Mr. Bridges' poetry is like Schubert's music [why Schubert's?]. If we like it, there is no more to be said. . . . If we do not like it, there is no more to be said either.' Put that in your pipe, 'Penguin,' and cease to complain of the state of literary criticism. Whether we like a thing or not, there is no more to be said. Criticism is superflous. Appreciation or the want of it is all. (*NA*, 15, 597, 1914.)

The Cocoon [a periodical discussed in the preceding week's column] was from Cambridge, the 'nursery of the nation'; this week we are at Oxford with *A Queen's College Miscellany for 1920*. And I hope that none of my readers will think that in considering the immature work and early exercises of writers still in the nursery we are wasting our time. 'To see things in the germ—that I call intelligence,' said a Chinese sage; and it is, moreover, sometimes easier to detect qualities in the green than in their ripeness. . . .

Let us consider the verse contained in the miscellany. Mr. Edmund Blunden has a long poem entitled 'Leisure,' and a typical stanza runs as follows:

> And the old hedger with his half-moon hook,
> Plashing the black thorn, musing of by-gone men,
> Shakes the crab-apples plopping in the brook
> Till jangling wild-geese flush from the drowned fen.

The observation of nature has plainly been very full, and many of the phrases are happily truthful. 'Plashing' and 'plopping' are perfectly appropriate; and the whole poem is of a similarly close texture. But it is, nevertheless, all to no purpose. When the pictures have been drawn, nothing remains except the feeling that follows the turning over of the leaves of a photographic album. 'That's nice,' you say; and having continued to say 'That's nice' or 'That's pretty' to a few score small landscapes, you yawn and put the album aside completely bored. The reason is that there is no *interest* in pictures merely as pictures. Without some powerful appeal to the mind, the final source of æsthetic emotion, even the most beautiful things in the world have no real interest for us. It is mind alone that creates interest; and since in Mr. Blunden's verse mind is missing, his pictures end by actually displeasing us. Such observation and such happy truthfulness of description ought not, however, to be allowed to have that effect; it is a shame to waste them. And I would suggest to Mr. Blunden that he employ them in eclogues or even in a great English poetic Nature-play. He has the raw material in his mind; now is needed the high aim of art. . . .

What do they read at our universities, those 'nurseries of the nation'? One of my best spiritual monitors informs me that on the barbarous Continent, and universally in Russia, every university student who studies literature, be it only with the ambition to become a journalist, includes, first and foremost, in his reading the great scriptures of the Aryan race: not only the Greek and Latin, but the Indian, the Zoroastrian, the Scandinavian; in general, the 'Sacred Books of the East.' And, next to them, he makes himself acquainted with the most recent researches designed to recover for our generation the inspiration of our racial sources. The mere 'literary' history of Europe, since the Renaissance, is only the interval between the highest culture of the past and the highest culture of the future. Neither in the present Oxford *Miscellany* nor in the Cambridge *Cocoon* which I unwound last week have I been able to find a trace of either culture. . . . Their models are all late Victorian or early Georgian; and their destination appears to me to be, at its highest, 'middles' in *The Spectator* or, at its worst, aimless, futile, precious 'magazines of art.' (*NA*, 27, 343-4, 1920.)

The Literary Kinds
and the Media

Although many critics call attention to the priority of oral to written literature, few of them pursue the consequences of the distinction. When writing is substituted for speaking, according to Orage, a certain deformation of language is necessary to incorporate effects that in speech are conveyed through inflection and gesture. The result is 'style'—the printed trace of the man. One of the dangers of script is that it may lead authors to cut themselves off from the oral sources of literature (*cf.* section 24). In a passage written in 1932, Orage looked to the wireless as a means of restoring the primacy of speech in cultural communication.

Orage thought that drama was the greatest of the literary kinds (*NA*, 9, 58, 1911) but was critical of the realistic plays of his time. He was one of the first socialist critics to resist the subordination of æsthetic to documentary and political aims in the drama. The Edwardian period proved to be the false dawn of what many writers hoped would be a dramatic renaissance; the following selections chart the gradual decline of the drama in its competition with the cinema. For Orage's later discussion of dramatic improvization, see 'A Theatre for Us,' *Little Review*, 11, 30–2, 1926.

A good many of the obscurities of literary criticism or the judgment of writing would be removed if only it were remembered that literature is a substitute for speech. Ages before the invention of script, men communicated with each other in the medium of words, and not on everyday occasions and everyday subjects only, but on special occasions and upon subjects of the whole range of human interest. For these special occasions, moreover, the form of the spoken communication was adapted both in respect of subject and style. Occasions of entertainment necessitated light and easy narrative forms, varying in length from the conte to the histoire. Historic occasions called for recollections in the form of biography, episode and epic. Solemn occasions or occasions of crisis demanded the religious narrative, intercession or ceremony, or appeals of the nature of oratory. There is scarcely a literary form now existing that was not cultivated and brought to a high degree of perfection ages before the invention of letters and the printing press.

However much else has been changed by the invention of a script for speech, it is obvious that the natural, original and fundamental relationship of ancient illiterate times differs in no important respect from the writer-reader relationship of literate ages. Now, as then, on the one side is a man employing words for the purpose of communicating his thoughts and feelings to others; and now, as then, on the other side are men predisposed by the fact of their presence and attention to receive and to be affected by the thoughts and feelings thus communicated to them. That this ancient relationship stands, indeed, fundamentally unchanged by all the changes due to printing is proved by this alone: that writing is everywhere acknowledged to be at its highest and best when it most closely reproduces the living presence of its author;—in short, when it speaks.

The judgment applied by hearers to speakers in the ages before printing was, however, an act rather than an art. No art-criticism, in fact, was needed in presence of the speaker himself. His hearers judged him exactly as they were in the instinctive habit of judging everybody else. He was forcible, he was grand, he was impressive, he was entertaining, in precisely the same way in which their own familiars were. Furthermore they had not to search the archives of his life for light upon his meaning. He was there before them in the flesh and everything he had to say was insensibly received by them in the light of his visible presence and personality. It was impossible to persuade them that they ought to give him their attention because of his reputation or the originality of his style or for any of the hundred and one reasons that an audience of hearers to-day is besought to read what is intrinsically distasteful. The ancients were all in this respect from Missouri; and the sight and sound of the speaker's living presence was the first and last criterion they employed for their judgment of the value of his communication. The man was the style.

Though, as I have said, the fundamental relationship remained unchanged with the introduction of printing, nevertheless the technique of the relationship has been greatly transformed. At opposite ends of the situation stand to-day the same two original figures, a speaker and a hearer; but, in place of the former direct and sensible communication between man and man, there is to-day the whole contrivance of printing; type has been substituted for voice.

At first glance it might appear that the difference thus introduced was merely mechanical, and that all that was needed was to record in script the words as uttered by the speaker. Naïve writers are still under the impression that a transcript of life is obtained by transcribing utterances textually. But this overlooks the fact that of the total presence of the speaker in person, his actual words are only a partial representation; and a thousand subtleties indiscoverable in the verbatim report of his speech were clearly perceived by his hearers in the light of his presence. Recall Æschines reading in exile the oration of Demosthenes that condemned him and deploring that it gave only a faint impression of its effect when Demosthenes delivered it. And Æschines was no mean orator himself. The transition from speaking to writing, from hearing to reading, demanded more, in short, than simply a script for the words; it demanded the addition to the verbal text of substitutes for all the rest of the living speaker's obvious properties, his gestures, his eyes, his movements, his whole personality. The conveyance, within the verbal framework of literature, of the man himself, apart from and over and above his mere words, is what is truly defined as style. In literature, the style is the man.

Unfortunately, with all our reading, the majority of readers are still naïve in their judgments of the man as revealed in his work. Though in truth there is always a man behind the work—be the work of any literary form—but in addition to being behind the work, he is also, by the agency of style, within the work as well, yet, thanks to the fact that our judgment of a man as writer is not instinctive like our judgments of men as men, but requires to be cultivated precisely because the style in question is necessarily cultivated, readers who would not be deceived as hearers for a single moment go hopelessly wrong in their judgment of speakers when disguised as writers. Not only are they carried away in the effects of the text upon themselves, but their true judgment of the value and significance of the writer as man is lost—sometimes never to be found—in their inability to look for the man in his work. ('Introduction,' *The Art of Reading*, New York, 1930, pp. ix–xii.)

20 Oratory (1915)

The volume under my hand is the latest in the admirable series I am always praising—the Oxford edition of the World's Classics at a shilling a volume. It is *Selected Speeches on British Foreign Policy* from Chatham to Sir Edward Grey. There are some twenty or thirty speeches and they run in all to over five hundred pages. Mr. Edgar Jones has edited them and, as he explains in a brief preface, his choice has been determined rather by the historical than by the oratorical value of the speeches he has drawn upon. At the same time they illustrate well enough the character of British oratory—its rise and, I was going to say, its decline. Compare, for example, the speech with which the volume concludes—the speech on 'International Honour' by Mr. Lloyd George, delivered last September—with the speech which opens the volume, that of Chatham upon the Convention with Spain, delivered in 1738. The gulf between them in the matter of style is Avernian. Mr. Lloyd George has fallen, as no other leading statesman of to-day has fallen, into the short sentences, the hot little enthusiasms, the clap-trap sentimentalities of the descriptive journalist. Plainly the man reads a disproportionate amount of newspaper, so that his style is out of the highroad of English tradition and in the byelane and blind alley of the Harmsworth mode. On the other hand, the speech by Mr. Asquith on the 'Infamous Proposals' is not altogether unworthy of a place in a volume with Pitt and Palmerston and Canning. . . .

Of all our English political speakers I am inclined to give the palm to Pitt. His style, while it was practical as being responsibly concerned with the question in hand, had just that concealed emotion which lifted the minds of his hearers without ever once breaking down their natural crust of reserve. Nobody, I think, ever wept during one of Pitt's speeches; nobody was made to feel creepy or was unmanned. For such breaches of the decorum we never really forgive a speaker. We have our revenge upon him, for having betrayed us, by calling him theatrical. Pitt was never theatrical or only upon the most rare occasions. Burke, on the other hand, with so much greater a mind, laboured under two disadvantages: he was usually on a wild-goose chase—in other words, it was usually a foregone conclusion against which he addressed himself; and secondly, he never understood or wholly sympathized with the English mind; he was English by art rather than by nature. Otherwise I confess it is inexplicable that neither Pitt nor Grenville thought his great speech on the Nabob of Arcot's Debts worth a reply. They kept their seats when Burke sat down, and said nothing. Then, too, Burke was obviously laborious. He delivered speeches of model rather than of use. Between him and Pitt there is the same difference as I find between Milton's 'old man eloquent,' and Desmosthenes. Isocrates wrote speeches in the style of Demosthenes, it is true; they are even, from a sedentary point of view, superior in form and phrasing. But the speeches of Demosthenes set Isocrates' virtues moving, and moving towards an end. Isocrates was writing for his reputation; Desmosthenes spoke for his life. And there, perhaps, we come upon the distinction between oratory and rhetoric. It is determined, as the dividing lines in all the arts between the major and the minor are determined, by the critical appreciation of the common people. Yes, the common people! Oh, you fancy, no doubt, you Parliamentary, Royal Academy, Mayoral Banquet and other specialized orators, that, provided your own select audience is exigent of style, you are secure of a high level or, at least, of a high pitch. But such select audiences are ruinous unless the people out of doors are invisibly present and silently appreciative. Demosthenes used to say that he owed his style to the Athenian mob. And what a style! I have just read again the speech 'For the Crown' (you can buy it in 'Everyman' for a shilling). Here is a man pleading for his life—talking dangerously, as Nietzsche would have men live dangerously—yet insinuating into his plea all his political appeals and carrying on his life-long propaganda while walking the tight-rope of a criminal trial. Even Aeschines, his prosecutor, was moved to admiration by it. In exile at Rhodes, where he established the Asiatic school of oratory, he used first to recite his own speech of indictment, and when his pupils could not imagine how it could be answered, he would recite to them the reply of Demosthenes. Cicero tells the story that on one occasion, when Aeschines had delivered the speech of Demosthenes to the admiration of all, he

added: 'Ah, but what would you have thought if you had heard the
man himself!' I would not like to improve modern oratory at the
expense of the re-institution of actual ostracism. If the arts cannot
flourish without physical violence, let them die! But I would
certainly make it as much as a man's *public* life was worth to deliver a
speech like many of Mr. Lloyd George's. It is, however, not a
matter in which a few only of us can have any immediate effect.
Though I should prove by analysis that his speech in this volume is
affected and false from beginning to end, the weight of ignorant
numbers would still sustain Mr. George's reputation until posterity
appears on the scene. I will not do it. Rather I will read Demosthenes
again. (*NA*, 16, 313–14, 1915.)

What of Shaw?

My attitude to him is precisely what Aristophanes' was to Euripides. Has it occurred to you to ask why Aristophanes preferred Aeschylus and Sophocles? It was not because these latter were better dramatic craftsmen than Euripides. Quite the contrary. Euripides is much superior technically. It was because Euripides was an inferior artist in that he was unable to put a soul into his plays. For a soul he substituted an idea. The descent was rapid. An idea became a political moral notion. Euripides in a decade after Sophocles' death was down among the propagandists. Shaw is there still.

Man and Superman, however, Shaw distinctly informs us is a religious play.

'A daw's not reckoned a religious bird because he cries from a steeple.' Shaw may affirm the religious character of his work until his face is as black as parson's cloth; but only New Theologians, that is, old Agnostics, will believe him. A genuine impulse to the soul is the sovereign virtue of religion; and what impulse do Shaw's plays give? To vote Progressive is as high a resolution as they compel. Can you imagine a solemn function being made of either Shaw or of Euripides? At the representation of the plays of Aeschylus and Sophocles at Athens there presided the Chief Archon, with the high priests of Dionysos and Apollo in stately symbolic attendance. Fancy that for a play concerning the evils of prostitution, or a new theory of evolutionary ethics! The proper place for these things is the lecture room or the market square; and their fitting audience consists of sociologists. But they have nothing to do with the soul. Social problems will not survive the death of the body as the soul does. Poverty and prostitution are not immortal.

It seems to me that you are repudiating the whole theory of the social utility of drama. If the drama, as Bernhardt told Arnold, is irresistible, why not employ its force to regenerate society?

If I deny that art has any definable utility, you must not conclude that I deny utility to it of any kind. But its service is not social, nor is it material. I even doubt the purity of any play that impels to any action, thought or idea in particular. From the sacrament of the Mass what think you a good Catholic would expect to derive in the way of ideas? He knows by an incommunicable but nevertheless indubitable experience that his soul has been nourished by participation in the ceremony. That is enough. 'Is it not enough?' Art is no less sacramental. I repeat that the drama is a religious ceremony and concerns the immortal soul. When it has not these attributes, you may call it drama if you please. I call it mummery.

You set dramatists a great task if they are to create a Mass every time they write a play. But do you really think the public would appreciate such drama?

I'm afraid I have misled you in mentioning the Mass. You should know that there are as many kinds of Mass as there are types of the soul and its adventures. The Church has but one; Art has a thousand. And not all the adventures of the soul are gloomy or solemn. There is the adventure of comedy as well as of tragedy. Once find your dramatist to whom the soul is known, he will discover variety enough in its history. But, as you agree, since Ibsen died where is the dramatist who is not a materialist? Or still worse, an ignoramus respectably disguised as an Agnostic or New Theologian. ('Unedited Opinions,' *NA*, 9, 58, 1911.)

You all appear to me unnecessarily severe on modern drama, particularly on what is called advanced drama. I have never understood why.

Not more severe than the public, do you think? What can be more severe critically than for the public to desert the theatre and flock in thousands to music-halls and cinemas, whither, indeed, drama is compelled to follow them, begging for a living? As for our reasons, would you really like to know them?

Indeed I would.

I need not go beyond one: the modern advanced drama is not drama at all, it is aimless discussion from the dramatic point of view.

But I gathered that your complaint of it was exactly the opposite— namely, that it had an aim. Propagandist, you dismissed it.

The aim of conviction, however, is not a dramatic aim, since in that case there is nothing to prevent oratory or reasoning or pleading or exposition from being called dramatic. Even popularly none of these modes is regarded as dramatic. Nor do they become dramatic by being displayed in a theatre instead of in the lecture-hall or the law court. I repeat that, from the dramatic point of view, the advanced dramas are aimless—they miss the mark of drama.

What is that mark, if I may ask?

Action—first, last, and always. Without action there is no drama. Essentially a drama is all action and nothing else. In the perfect play (which, by the way, has never been written) action would be the sole content.

No words, no scenery—all dumb show?

That would be pantomime, not drama. Of course there would be words. But they, too, would form a part of the action. The dialogue itself would be dramatic.

But I do not understand how a dialogue differs from a discussion. The modern advanced drama presents discussion in dialogue form. Why is not that dramatic?

I will tell you. It is not solely designed to elucidate the action; nor is it designed solely to elucidate the character. Its main purpose is to elucidate the subject. And this purpose, I contend, is dialectical, not dramatic. Plato employed that method and properly, he being a dialectician; but he would never profess that his dialogues were dramatic, even though you should put them on the stage. To reproduce the circumstances of a discussion is not drama, however interesting such a representation might be, since the problem for the spectator would be an intellectual and not a dramatic one.

That distinction again! And I have not yet grasped it.

Yet it is not difficult. Let me ask you: When you act are you always aware of all your motives? Sometimes you think you are, sometimes you know you are not. Now consider the occasions when you are *not* aware of all your motives—what induces you then to act?

Instinct, I suppose, or the disposition and habits of my own nature.

In other words, forces which lie beneath your rational comprehension, and are neither rational nor irrational, but simply non-rational?

Very likely.

Well, the mystery of action obviously lies there. Actions that we can rationalize, explain, forecast, determine, are actions motived by the reasoning brain. With them drama has nothing to do, for drama is the representation of a mystery. What economy of art would drama display if actions already intelligible were embraced in her province? Drama begins where reason leaves off. The office of drama is to throw a light on what otherwise would remain a mystery. Even then, however, the mystery does not become intellectually intelligible. It is not the province of drama to explain, but only to illuminate. Nobody, for example, should profess to be able, after Shakespeare's plays, to understand Lear or Othello. But to be made aware of the existence of the hidden forces of passion, to be made to feel them—that is to have been subjected to drama.

Then reason, you say, gives place in drama to passion?

Precisely; for passion is that activity of the will which escapes the articulate consent of the brain. Whatever can be said is rational, and may or may not lead to action. Passion, on the other hand, is—directly—speechless; words utterly fail it, because words are not its language. The language of reason is speech; the language of passion is action.

But no play can exist on action alone, as we were agreeing. If drama is composed of passion, and passion can only be expressed by action, words of any kind are a superfluity. Is there no contradiction in this?

There would be if we confine action to its last and visible manifestations. But drama differs from pantomime in this, that it represents not only the final outcome of passion, but its subterranean, preparatory and premonitory workings. Pantomime, for instance, can represent only the ripened act as it appears: in bodily form. Drama, on the contrary, represents this act in its spiritual development within the soul, and is even disposed to omit the representation of the material outermost, and, so to say, pantomimic act altogether. Banquo, you will remember, was not murdered on the stage, though his murder was the final outcome of the passions that had been represented.

And this premonitory preparatory activity you would allow to be the province of words in drama?

Yes, dramatic conversation, as I call it, is always aiming, as it were, at pantomime, but always just stopping short of it. It brings you to the threshold of the brain and there leaves you to reason as you please. Its work is done when its pupils have been conducted safe into their own world.

Their own world being the rationally conscious as distinct from the unrational sub-conscious?

You have hit it exactly. Drama is the representation and therewith the illumination of the sub-conscious. We are made to *feel* that we understand, though we are aware that our understanding cannot be expressed in words. The sub-conscious element in drama appeals to the sub-conscious element in us. Deep calleth unto deep.

Are there any modern dramatists in this sense of the word?

Ibsen, in his later plays, I think; though few people realize how profoundly they differ from his earlier plays. His earlier plays had perfect technique in respect of dialogue, however. See how he denies his characters a single word that does not carry the action of their passion forward. In their conversation he traces the lines along which you can follow the currents of their will as they move and converge and gather into a volume of resolution. But for the most part, the contemplated and destined action is trivial in his earlier plays. Only in his later plays does the action become profound and symbolic. But I fancy we shall never get the perfect drama until we have created the perfect stage—the nature of which Mr. Huntly Carter, alone among critics, appears to know. I confess I have learned it from him.

And what is it?

He is of *The New Age*, ask him. But I may describe it in my own words. First, however, let me explain in what respect the present theatre is deficient for the purpose of drama. With the stage placed as it is, the audience is not made to realize the identity of the persons of the play with itself. Actually, the stage is only the specially illuminated area in which the audience beholds, as in a vision, its own passions represented. They should conceive the actors as merely figures of their own sub-conscious selves. As at a successful Quaker meeting the spirit of the assembly seizes first one and then the other of its members and speaks through them so that the audience goes away understanding itself better—at a successful dramatic representation the audience regards the actors as acting and speaking for them. Well, the position of the modern stage makes this illusion difficult. The actors appear to speak and act *to* their audience, not for them. The wrong attitude on the part of both actors and audience is encouraged. But suppose that the stage were placed in the very midst of the audience—the theatre being round and the stage being its centre—the play would then appear more readily as the sub-conscious mind of the audience made visible. Intimacy would be established. . . . But Mr. Carter must explain the rest himself. ('Unedited Opinions,' *NA*, 10, 371–2, 1912.)

22 Cinema (1917)

I have recently been to a cinema exhibition, and I was not a little surprised by the contrast it presented with the moving pictures I saw some ten or eleven years ago. Then, I remember, the exhibition was extremely crude but surprisingly interesting for the length, at any rate, of half an hour. One saw scenery photographed from a moving train, rivers from source to mouth, panoramas of cities and the like. It was a vivid geography lesson. In the cinema of to-day, to judge by my recent experience, one seldom sees any of these instructive things. The programme is designed to amuse, to thrill, to interest, but never to instruct. . . .

Theatre-managers of my acquaintance complain to me of the decadence of the age as exhibited in the gradual conversion of theatres into picture palaces. Half a dozen London theatres that once provided material for the wit of my colleague are now emptied of drama and filled with cinema-pictures. Half the profession is already exclusively engaged in acting for the cinema, and the other half is getting ready to take to the films instead of the boards at the first opportunity. Writers (I will not call them dramatists) who used to write for the legitimate now write for the machine; and even the writers who still aim at the boards have the screen in their mind as their final ambition. . . .

Not only is the cinema here to stay, but it is here to stay on its present lines. The world is neither going to get tired of it and return it to the schools, nor has invention ceased with the complicated films recently exhibited at one of the fashionable galleries in the presence of a number of distinguished persons, including men of taste as well as of curiosity. The answer to the question to what best possible use the cinema may be put is therefore not that it be restored to the use of science, but that it be developed for the use of people in general. But what is that use? This involves, in the first place, the reply to the question whether the cinema can ever command the attention of the intelligent as a form of art, to which I answer that in the nature of things it never can; for I agree with my colleague that the cinema is no more an instrument of art than a barrel-organ or a pianola. In the second place, however, since, if there are to be pianolas and cinemas, it is as well that they should be the best possible of their kind, my answer is that the best use of the cinema is to develop it upon its present lines until it becomes, if not elevating to the intelligent, at least not corrupting to the unintelligent. To art we look for the perfectioning of the person; let us, at any rate, see that artifice does not ruin the populace.

The broad distinction between the cinema and the drama or the cinema and the novel is similar to the distinction between the picture-paper and the journal of views. In each case the former appeals mainly to the eye in the form of pictures, while the latter appeals to the mind. To take my own profession, that of journalism, if I were asked if the picture-paper has had any effect upon the views-journal, I should reply that it has had, on the whole, a good effect. It has drawn off from the audience we journalists used to address all the mere creatures of sense-impressions, and has left us free to develop views for an ever-increasing audience of intellectuals. No doubt about it whatever—a journal like *The New Age* owes its existence to reaction from the world that takes the picture-papers; and, in time to come, papers like *The New Age* will increase in numbers and flourish. By analogy, I think that the drama and the novel may likewise profit by the cinema; for the cinema, if it is properly developed, will draw off from the drama and the novel precisely those elements that are actually superfluous in those arts.

Before the cinema came, the tendency of plays was in the direction of the picturesque; witness the late Sir Herbert Tree, a cinema-artiste before his time. But now that the cinema has come, this tendency may be checked and finally destroyed; and with its destruction the play of character, of psychology, and of the spoken word may come to be written again. (*NA*, 21, 488–9, 1917.)

23 Radio (1932)

Already the radio has a larger circulation than any newspaper, and very soon, there is little doubt, its circulation will be greater than that of all the newspapers put together. Is that not certain to subordinate the press to the radio as an engine for the formation of public opinion? And must not the press in consequence take a back seat to the radio? What is more, I do not see any possible improvement in the press to give it a hope of triumph over its rival. The stage always had, and still has, a unique virtue to exploit that would have left the cinema panting somewhat ridiculously behind it. I cannot imagine, for instance, that the Greek dramatists would have been much perturbed by the competition of such a rival; or that Shakespeare and the Elizabethans, had they been alive to-day, would not have 'thought of something' with which to ensure the supremacy of the stage. The triumph of the cinema over the stage, in fact, has been and is due less to the difference of their intrinsic values than to the superiority of the brains put into the cinema over those put into the stage. But in the case of the newspaper press, it has not, I think, a tuck to run out like the stage. It has no great past of which to make a great future. Its present will prove, I believe, to be its greatest past, and its future will be a slow decline in relation to the rapid rise of the radio. For radio, it is certain, is only in its mighty beginning. . . .

With a little real imagination, it is not difficult to establish something like a parallel between what is happening to-day and what happened when letters were first invented. Before the ingenious Kadmus, or whoever it was, devised a script for the recording of speech, men had for thousands of years been content to be speakers and hearers. Their speech, moreover, was not confined to the commonplaces of daily life; it was cultivated as an art. And there is plenty of evidence to prove that in every form of verbal composition, the predecessors of the 'Yankee' invention of script created master-

pieces with which, as yet, no written substitutes can compare. . . .
Script, however, won in the end,—to the loss of human culture.
The machine triumphed, and with its triumph the great traditions of
improvisation in the speech of man and in all the provinces of the
art of words,—narrative, oratory, poetry, drama—(for it must be
remembered that even drama was improvised before the relatively
decadent days of the scriptorial Greeks),—all came to an end.
For the speaker there was substituted the writer, and for the hearer
the reader, with such corruptions of integrity and judgment on
both sides that even to-day after two thousand years of its use the
written word is more often a source of mutual misunderstanding
than of common understanding. In two thousand years there have
been scarcely a dozen literary critics as good as any 'hearer' of the
days before script. Still, to-day, the printing machine 'puts across'
writers who, as speakers, would not have been given a first, let alone
a second, hearing; and still, to-day, not one reader in a million
'listens' to the printed word as if it were, what it is, a man speaking
through a machine, and to be judged as a man speaking. It is possible that the radio, by partially if not completely restoring the
original relationship of speaker, listener, may at the same time improve both writing and reading. Unless, in fact, it does, I can see
literature going the way of the stage and of the press. (*NEW*, 1,
138–9, 1932.)

Victorian and Edwardian Literature

Orage's literary column in *The Labour Leader*, 1895-7, is discussed briefly in the Introduction. In his column in *The New Age* he had occasion to discuss Victorian authors only when their works were republished. His references to his own experience of the literary milieu of the 1890s, some of which are included in this section, are of biographical as well as critical interest. By 1913, Shaw, Wells, and Bennett had already written the works for which they are best known to-day; most of his paragraphs on them and on the Victorians that he discussed in 'Readers and Writers' are included in *The Art of Reading*.

For a discussion of the controversy between Henry James and H. G. Wells concerning the form of the novel, which is reflected in the following selections, see *Henry James and H. G. Wells*, edited by Leon Edel and Gordon N. Ray, London, 1958. Wells discussed James and included a few unflattering references to Orage in *Boon*, 1914.

From Edward FitzGerald to
Aestheticism (1913, 1918, 1932)

Omar Khayyam has not now the vogue he had in England twenty
years ago. In those days most of us knew our Fitzgerald by heart
and wallowed in the sentimental self-pity induced by his rhythms. I
am told and can well believe that whatever the sentimental content
of the original, the spirit as expressed in the form, is translated by
Fitzgerald only in Bottom's sense, that is, it is metamorphosed. It
came, however, as an opportune reaction to the discovery that
science, even Tennysonian science, was bankrupt. Spencer and
Darwin had mechanized the world and carried the industrial
revolution into thought. Tennyson on his lawn had prettified it and
hung it with paper garlands. But nothing could conceal the fact that
the new world was repellant and that *nothing* was better than the
only certainty promised by it. In this nihilistic rebound we were
all carried away, and Fitzgerald's 'Omar' led us. But our courage
has long since returned, and the spectres of Spencer and Tennyson
are now no more than historic turnip-heads. I do believe that at this
moment Spencer and Tennyson are two of the most despised of the
great English writers. They are proved to have frightened us without
cause or to have attempted to soothe us without reality; and for the
double offence the pair cannot be forgiven this century. With our
courage returned also our good sense, and in the light of good sense
Omar Khayyam ceased to be the refuge of despair. We can, I hope,
all laugh at him now; not, of course, with contempt, for we do not
know that we may not have to fly to him again; but with good humour.
(*NA*, 14, 240, 1913.)

[Concerning J. M. Kennedy's *English Literature, 1880–1905* and
Holbrook Jackson's *The Eighteen Nineties:*] Melancholy, in Mr.
Kennedy's opinion, was the keynote of the last generation of English
literature; and this was due, he suggested, to 'the vogue of philosophies which tended to set the reason above the imagination.' The

phrase itself is a product of our own time, but the change is at least as old as the contemporaries of Socrates. I set no store myself by such easy psychological explanations that explain nothing. How came it, for example, that reason mastered imagination, if so it did? And why under similar circumstances had we the so classic literature of the eighteenth century? The yellow melancholy of the eighteen-nineties had an origin, I believe, less philosophical than sociological. The same years that saw the début of Wilde saw also the début of the Independent Labour Party. A first-rate critic of the period would discover the common origin of both. Mr. Jackson, as a sometime Socialist himself, is dimly aware that the two phenomena were related; and at one point he begins to investigate their cause. The literature of this period was concerned, he says, 'with the idea of social life'; but he immediately abandons the quest in adding: '*or, if you will, of culture.*' (My italics.) But I will not! I will not accept social life and culture as convertible terms, more especially since in the same paragraph Mr. Jackson re-defines the 'idea' of the period as 'a determination to taste new sensations for the sake of personal development.' The self-contradiction of this paragraph is something neither rational nor imaginative; it is simply carelessness. If the idea of the 'nineties was social life, it could not at the same time be personal sensation; unless, as I believe is the fact, the period had both ideas and each at war with the other.

Having been myself both a student of Pater and an early member of the ILP I happen to remember the 'feel' of the period under review very well; for along with others I was more truly its embodiment than any of the more prominent writers of those days. Melancholy, I can most truly say, was not at the outset the badge of our tribe, nor was the passion for 'social life.' Our social reformatory zeal was not allowed to interfere with our pursuit of personal 'moments' of choice sensation; nor, on the other hand, did we imagine that the latter would interfere with the former. The point, however, to observe is that it did! And melancholy was quite naturally the result for a while of one or other choice. There were those, for example, who in the choice between personal and social idealism chose the former; there were those likewise who chose the latter; I am thankful to say that I was one of them. Of the first set the end was in almost every instance one of melancholy, of decadence, suicide, or premature death. They had cut themselves off from society hoping to blossom on a stem cut off from the trunk of the tree; and they withered away. Of the second set it is not for me to speak. These things, however, can be said of them, that they thrust hedonism behind them, abjured Pater and his whole school, and plunged into the waters of what Mr. Kennedy superciliously calls democracy. It remains to be seen whether, after this cleansing elemental bath, this return to simple truths, simple words, and simple life, we shall, as I hope, recover an art at once national and individual. (*NA*, 14, 50, 1913.)

I well remember the sensations—they were hardly to be called ideas—the successive quarterly volumes [of *The Yellow Book*] aroused in us, that is to say, in those of my contemporaries who were then mewing their literary youth. From the twice-breathed air of the conventional literature of the day we used to turn into *The Yellow Book* much as one escapes to-day from a crowd in Kew Gardens into the palm-house or the conservatory where they grow wonderful orchids. The atmosphere was oppressive and sultry; it was what we have since learned to call precious; but as a change from the workaday and somewhat knockabout air out of doors it was pleasant and not, certainly, altogether unprofitable. . . .

Literary periods do not come and go by accident; nor do schools rise and fall without rhyme or reason. The future—the brief and inglorious future—of *The Yellow Book* was implied in the very standards of goodness adopted by its editor. In a word, the purely æsthetic standard was certain in its nature to bring about an early decay. . . . A cul-de-sac occurs in literary history when a direction is taken away from the main highway of the national language and literature; when the stream it represents is not part of the main stream of the traditional language, but a back-water or a side stream. There have been dozens of such private streams in the course of our literary history; and I am not denying for an instant that their final contribution to the main stream has been considerable. Only reflect on the variety of 'influences' to which English literature has been indebted; and it will be found, I have no doubt, that each of them owed its origin to a school of a particular goodness whose own end was as lamentable as that of *The Yellow Book*. My point, therefore, is not at all that the school of *The Yellow Book* was without merit or that it did not bring home something to the main stream of its day. (That point is for subsequent debate.) All I contend is that in itself it led nowhere or only upon the rocks of realism or into the shallows of fancifulness; and its pioneers were therefore compelled either to turn back or to perish. (*NA*, 23, 397–8, 1918.)

The '92's, with Walter Pater as the grand initiator, inaugurated a movement in literature not at all in the line of its previous most happily and most naturally established true development towards an always unattainable but an ever nearer identification with speech, but in a direction away from speech into what then began to be called pure literature, literature, that is to say, which aims to become not speech but words. The 'decadent' movement of the '92's was actually, in my judgment, the beginning of our present end. Under the impulse given it by Pater—who, be it remembered, wrote English as if it were a foreign language,—literary English began to get further and further away from its natural source and model. To use a violent image constantly employed by America's great living poet-critic, Mr. Robinson Jeffers, written words, after Pater, began to become 'incestuous' and to breed among themselves. Instead of keeping their minds on the unheard discourse of perfect speech, and trying in vain but ever more nearly to write down what their inner if not outer ear heard, writers began making patterns among their written words, allowing one to suggest another, mating them to-gether, quite indifferent to their natural relations, by their literary and even their literal associations. The result has been that literature since the '92's has been increasingly sterile in its contact with life. Few writers to-day can produce the effects of speech; and fewer still either unconsciously or consciously aim to do so. Apart from journalism whose language is a bastard of books and the street, most of the written word of to-day is a product of words upon words, books upon books. And it is, without doubt, the most unfruitful age of English literature in respect of its influence upon life. Even unfruitful, unfortunately, is not the truth about it; for its fruit in life is the manifestation of the epicene. (*NEW*, 1, 329, 1932.)

25 Neglected Edwardians (1914)

I have frequently in these columns indicated subjects for criticism which on no account ought to be shirked by contemporaries. The works of Mr. Allen Upward, for example, positively invite the large-minded and courageous critic. Here is, as I said, a phenomenon of a most paradoxical character from which have proceeded, during the last fifteen years, works of such mutual inconsistency as *The New Word*—a tour de force in philosophy—*Secrets of the Courts of Europe*—superior *Strand Magazine* melodramas; rubbishy articles in *The Egoist* and elsewhere on current politics; and *The Divine Mystery*—a scholarly treatise on religious folk-lore. The same author, I believe, has in manuscript or in mind, at least a score of other works of a no less mixed nature—including poems, plays, a digest of English law, a work on primitive Christianity and a Utopia. What are his contemporaries doing, I ask, to let a man like this pass comparatively unnoticed? Amongst all the realists with their eyes professedly glued on the current moment surely one is capable of posing and attempting to solve the problem of Allen Upward! For a problem manifestly is there. Mind, I do not say that it is a great problem or that the solution will prove pleasing either to Mr. Upward or to our epoch. But it is an unsolved problem and we ought not to leave more of these than we can help to those who will come after us.

Mr. Grierson, I do not hesitate to say, is another problem of a not altogether dissimilar nature. What *is* the truth about this extraordinary personality and writer? Somebody ought certainly to make a comprehensive and final study of him. Sometimes I am convinced that he is one of the great charlatans of literature, a writer with nothing original to say, but with an impressive manner of borrowing. At other times I am disposed to give him credit for one of the rarest qualities in literature, namely, atmosphere. Read, for instance, chapters XI and XII of *The Valley of Shadows* and deny,

I

if you can, that the air of genuine tragedy is created. But it is as an essayist that Mr. Grierson challenges valuation; and in this aspect the critic's task ought to be easy. Yet nobody has attempted it that I can discover—not, that is, on the large scale indispensable to a final judgment. Other critic-neglected writers whose names occur to me are Mr. J. W. Bain, of the Indian stories, Mr. W. H. Hudson, Mr. G. R. S. Mead, Mr. Barry Pain, Mr. Oliver Onions, Mr. Marmaduke Pickthall. . . . Has anybody read competent essays on any of these? But why are they not written? Some publisher ought to commission a volume of *Studies in Neglected Contemporaries*.

Of studies of Shaw, Chesterton, etc., we have more than enough. Every timid little scribbler can safely write his appreciation or criticism of these, for by this time every opinion possible of them has been well trodden. Editors tell me that their average of manuscripts about Messrs. Shaw and Chesterton is half a dozen a week, which, on a fair estimate, means that fifty articles a week or over two thousand a year are being written on these two writers. What cowards essayists must be, and how dull! Thomas Hardy, I suppose, comes next, now that Meredith is dead; and shortly, no doubt, Henry James and Joseph Conrad will be suffering the tramp of a thousand feet. (*NA*, 14, 530, 1914.)

26 H. G. Wells (1897, 1913, 1915)

The Wheels of Chance . . . is realistic, it is comic, it is humourous, it is pathetic. Imagination plays not the same melodramatic part [that it did in his scientific fantasies], but there is more of sympathy and more of all the powers and feelings which make a writer great. . . . It takes a great amount of talent—almost enough to make genius—to put a draper's assistant in the middle of the canvas. H. G. Wells is a young man scarcely tried, and it was no common boldness which made him select what the world considers so unromantic a person. However, from first to last, our sympathies are with Hoopdriver. Ridiculous as Wells makes him, absurd and altogether comic as are his little arrogances and prides, the details are true to life. What is more, they are never caricatured or over-balanced; they are never touched with the chill finger of satire. (*The Labour Leader*, 29 May 1897, p. 178.)

It is in *The Athenæum* that Mr. Wells comes to his second grief—his first, I need not say, having met him in these columns. After some eulogistic flourishes to the effect that Mr. Wells is in the front rank of novelists (as who is not in these days?), *The Athenæum* coolly informs Mr. Wells that 'he has never cared to learn how to write.' What! a man can be in the front rank of a literary art and never have learned to write! From this judgment, however, I must dissent, for it is not true that Mr. Wells cannot write. What Mr. Wells cannot do is to re-write and to delete. Take, for example, the instances cited by *The Athenæum*—phrases like 'massive, ancient and traditional common way of living,' 'vast, enduring, normal human existence,' 'unlettered, laborious and essentially unchanging.' Such overblown phrases are no evidence that Mr. Wells cannot write; but they *are* evidence that he is too idle or too careless of his public to distil his thought for its essence. I am certain, however, that the blame of this is less Mr. Wells' than that of his public and the reviewers. Who, in his early days, when he was rising, put the fear of critics in him? Who ventured to withhold a superlative until he should have earned it? Who denied him golden spurs before he had run his course? The answer is Nobody. Thus the reviewers have themselves to blame for the comfortable, careless, contemptuous adiposity of Mr. Wells' present style. Despite of this bad habit, however, *The Athenæum* still bids Mr. Wells to produce his masterpiece. But what is the character of this to be? His most dangerous admirers will infallibly demand some monumental work of sociological significance—the sort Mr. Wells has already failed in more than once. Briefly, Mr. Wells knows no more of sociology than Mr. Bennett knows of life. His less dangerous admirers will ask for more scientific romances—but he has written his best of these and the field is exhausted. The present admirer would direct Mr. Wells' attention to sections 5, 6 and 7 of Chapter V of *Mr. Polly* or to the 'romance' in *The Wheels of Chance*. There, I believe, is Mr. Wells' rainbow, at the foot of which he will find his treasure. (*NA*, 13, 601, 1913.)

We may see in Mr. Wells' recent work the reductio ad absurdum of his anarchic theories of this literary form. Listen to him upon Mr. Henry James. 'James,' he says, 'has never discovered that a novel isn't a picture. He wants a novel to be simply and completely *done*. He wants it to have a unity; he demands homogeneity.... But if the novel is to follow life it must be various and discursive.' Who demanded that the novel should 'follow' life? No artist, it is certain. 'Leading' life is more the way of the creator. And, again, who, but Mr. Wells, disputes Mr. James' claim that a novel must be a unity and have homogeneity? The effect of Mr. Wells' theories is to be seen in contrast with the effects Mr. James produces. In the latter the illusion of life is preserved, but of life in selected aspects designed to exhibit a single mood or a single character. But in the former everything sprawls like the items in a daily paper. String on a thin running motive the contents of any issue of *The Times*, from 'Births, Deaths and Marriages' to 'Property Sales,' and the result is one of Mr. Wells' recent novels. And twopence is less than six shillings!

The morbid interest, however, is not confined to the form, it includes the leading characters of Mr. Wells' latest novels. I could believe that he was metamorphosed in Russia and has become a Russian, so similar are now his heroes to the painfully crucified protagonists of Russian literature. The 'harmony of will and deed' which we desire to establish, is in Mr. Wells' heroes a discord ever growing more depressing. They start off with dreams which only supermen could realize and find, after a chapter or two, that their author has equipped them with the character of moral imbeciles. What end is possible but suicide or subsidence into some corner of life? That such characters *appeared* to be common a year or two ago is an admission I make to Mr. Wells. There were, indeed, scores of young men in the pre-war days whose imagination stretched its neck miles beyond their forefeet. But it was an appearance only, as the war has proved. Mr. Wells has presumably taken an interest in the war and, professionally, in its reactions upon psychology. Where now, except in concealed literary circles, does he find his Benhams? And if there be any such, I doubt whether the stumbling-block is always sex. Sex, for Mr. Wells' later heroes, is the pons asinorum upon which they always come to grief. This is not the case with his Russian peers, who usually contrive a greater trial than physical sex. In this respect, therefore, Mr. Wells is worse than the Russians. However, it is all symptomatic, I dare say; and Mr. Wells is the infant of the passing age. These novels will pass with it. (*NA*, 17, 527, 1915.)

I have seen it written that Henry James was a greater psychologist than his brother William, and I have seen it denied with indignation. The dispute might have been saved by the true statement that, as psychologists, the two brothers were equally accomplished but in different fields. The field of William James was in the main the field of normal and of abnormal conscious psychology; the field of Henry James was the field of the sub-conscious, both normal and abnormal. The difference to those who know what the terms mean, is not only considerable; but it accounts entirely for the difference of method employed by the two brothers and even, to a great extent, for the difference in their modes of life. The conscious can be studied by the scientist in the laboratory; the material is, moreover, largely under his control; and all the ordinary rules of scientific research apply to it. But the sub-conscious is a shyer creature altogether. It is not susceptible of direct observation; it cannot be conjured up or laid at will; it must be watched, attended upon, and delicately, oh most delicately, observed; it entails a discipline of the imagination and of the senses, and a discipline of the mind of the observer who must beware of even so much as breathing in the presence of the subconscious subject; in a word, its study is much more an art than a science.

I am not suggesting that Henry James arrived by his method at any conclusions likely to be of value to the science of psychology. Conclusions were not what he aimed at; he aimed, like every author, at representation. Nor, again, am I suggesting that Henry James held intellectually any theories on the sub-conscious. He was, as it were, professionally inclusive and professionally open-minded. At the same time, it would be possible, I hold, to discover in the solution of his works quite definite conclusions and quite definite theories which the intellect might precipitate into the crystallized dust of formal definitions. But why attempt it if Henry

James himself did not? Why translate into terms of science a work of art? Why substitute for representation mere definitions? Only, if it be done, to convince his readers that they are really in the current of the most recent and the deepest thought of our day.

For the surprising thing about Henry James's novels is that one approaches them as stories and leaves them having assisted at a piece of life. One begins to read him as a diversion and finds at the end of him that one has had real experiences. He is, in fact, the magician of psychology, who not only describes—who, indeed does not describe, but portrays,—but reveals. He takes his readers through a new world. This marvellous magical gift, moreover, is exercised, like all true magic, by the simplest of means. For the most part Henry James's characters cannot be said to be selected for their extraordinariness; nor had he the accessories of the stage-magician for his properties. Quite ordinary people in quite ordinary surroundings are sufficient for his purpose—which is to show us, not the conscious, but the sub-conscious, in man. 'There,' he seems to say,—having placed his reader at a point of vantage for observation,—'just observe and listen and hold your mind in readiness to catch the smallest gesture and the lightest tone. These persons you will notice, are not at the first glance anything out of the common, nor are they up to anything very unusual. Nevertheless, watch them and try to see and to feel what they are doing!' And as his readers look at the figures through Henry James's eyes, they are aware of a strange transformation in the ordinary people before them. While still remaining ordinary, extraordinary manifestations begin to be visible among them. They arouse wonder, they arouse pity, they arouse admiration, they arouse horror or fear. There are few emotions they are not capable of producing under the wand of Henry James. Yet, all the time—I must insist upon it— these people remain ordinary.

Such an art of second-sight as this was not likely to be confined to the merely incarnated. If Henry James drew our attention to the sub-conscious 'double' or psychic penumbra of living figures, he was almost certain in the end to present his figures as doubles without a body, in a word, as ghosts. And I was among the critics who, long before Henry James had written his *Two Magics* prophesied that he would shortly be writing of shadows directly. No student of his works can fail to observe how imperceptibly his method of dealing with real persons shades into his dealing with ghosts. There is a little more quietness, a little more mystery, a little

more holding of the breath in the process of observation; but fundamentally the method is the same. His stories of the unembodied are,
I think, the flower of his art. In these Henry James rose to the
perfection of his observation. In them he examined the sub-
conscious, as it were, face to face.

I have remarked on another occasion that Henry James would
be happy among the dead, for he understood them while he was
still living. But let me supplement the remark here by the observation that Henry James did not commune with the disembodied
alone, but aloud and in the hearing and in the experience of all his
intended readers. His mission (if I may use the word and grieve
for it) was to act as a kind of Charon to ferry the understanding
over the dark passage of the Styx and to show us that we are such
stuff as ghosts are made of. ('Henry James and the Ghostly,' *The
Little Review*, 5, 41–3, 1918.)

Modern Literature

As discoverers of literary talent, Orage and Ford Madox Ford were the most successful English editors of the early twentieth century. They were both born in 1873 and in the eyes of the younger generation (D. H. Lawrence, Ezra Pound, Katherine Mansfield, Wyndham Lewis, Edwin Muir, and others whose works they published) they were less threatening than the father figures of the Victorian period, yet sufficiently old to quarrel with and to respect. That Ford and Orage looked for talent among the young and were able to recognize it is a tribute to their perspicacity and their freedom from the literary prejudices of their own generation.

The following selections show Orage attempting to understand the literature of his time and continually revising his estimate of its value as more evidence, in the form of more literary works, became available. He said little about authors whom he considered unimportant. The fact that he wrote at greater length about Pound, Joyce, and Wyndham Lewis than about other contemporary authors is indicative of his estimate of their significance, despite the fact that he is often critical of their work.

28 The Character of the Age (1914)

I often envy my colleague, the writer of the 'Notes of the Week,' the continuity of his dramatic and critical weekly commentary. Mine, in comparison, is a thing of shreds and patches with no particular relevance to any movement in the literary world. I have come to think, however, that the reason is not my fault, but the fault of the age. In the political and economic worlds there are, after all, definite schools of thought and definite currents of endeavour and tendency. It is comparatively easy (if I may say so) to dramatize these and to visualize them all as working out some vast plot. But what is there to correspond in the literary world? In the first place, there are practically no schools, but only cliques of writers personally but not spiritually related; secondly, no common problem is posed for practical solution; thirdly, there are no currents in literary opinion. Large criticism in such a world cannot possibly be consecutive, since there is no bond of unity among the various sets of writers. To-day somebody publishes a realistic novel; to-morrow somebody else publishes a romantic or an historical or a genre or a fantastic novel. How can they be related? I confess I cannot do it. (*NA*, 15, 62, 1914.)

Readers occasionally find fault with *The New Age* for apparently having no literary policy—as if you had only to sit down and imagine a policy and then proceed to expound it. But a policy is not arrived at in that way. That way lies idiosyncrasy. To formulate a true policy, two things are required—first, a good standard, and, secondly, a perceptible drift and tendency in one's age. While claiming to possess good standards, I affirm that our age is for the present too distracted and puzzled to have any particular tendency. Our writers are revolving very busily on their axes, and some, even, set off for somewhere; but who can say that so much as a school are going in the same direction? What, in fact, is *the* literary tendency of the age? Mr. Gosse has made a shot at an answer by defining it as 'the increased study of life in its exhibitions of energy'; and high marks should be given him, for his formula covers a good many of the phenomena. But, on the other hand, it does not cover all nor the most significant of existing literary phenomena. I do not remark, for instance, much study of energetics in current novels and plays— where, presumably, it should appear most clearly. On the contrary, our novels and plays are concerned with very supine people as a rule, as remote from exhibitions of astonishing energy as from ideals of any kind. In verse, perhaps, Mr. Gosse's case is a little stronger; for Mr. Masefield undoubtedly preaches energetics and, quite as undoubtedly, is somewhat of a fashion. But the fashion is fleeting and is, indeed, as good as obsolete; and the next boom was of Tagore, the least energeticomaniac of them all. I conclude, once more, that the age is really characterless; like Mr. Wells, it is versatile and nothing more. It will be recorded in history as doing everything badly. (NA, 14, 722, 1914.)

At a time when for the moment nothing new upon the old lines appears to be opening up . . . it is natural that writers and artists with no new vision into reality should turn their jaded and sophisticated minds back to what was undoubtedly the source of their first inspiration, namely, their childhood. But the childhood so evoked, and after all this world-weariness, is not the original childhood either of the individual or of the race. That is to say, its character is neither simple nor primitive; but, on the contrary, an affectation of both these qualities. For instance, Mr. Masefield's sanguinary melodramas in their hotchpotch setting of pastoral-cum-pothouse description are neither the tales of schoolboys nor the camp-fire tales of primitive hunters. As far as they are from modern life so far are they also from any life that ever was or ever will be lived. The same, in a slightly different sense, is true of Mr. Yeats' fairy-tales, which, in my experience, children dislike as much as I do; also of Tagore and Stephens, both of whom commit the crime of incongruously mixing the artful with the artless, the cynical with the naïve, the blasé with the childish. But this is only to say that the outstanding feature of the work of these men (and they are typical) is infantilism which, as I define it, is a compound of immaturity with decadence.

Before mentioning any names of corresponding situation in art, I may reply to a question that is sure to be raised. Assuming infantilism to be the prevailing vice, by what has it been produced and how can it be cured? About its causes there can, I think, be a doubt only concerning their number, whether it be many or few. Nobody will deny that what my colleague, Mr. Ludovici, calls 'a great order of society' is lacking in most men's minds to-day (even, I say with trembling, in Mr. Ludovici's). Our writers do not *think* from a settled background either of fact or of imagination. Actually either variety would serve the purpose of literature and art; the order of society that exists (if only it would stand still for five minutes) or an order in Utopia. But on neither have our writers any hold; and in consequence they flounder about alternately howling like dragons and wailing like babes. A second cause is the rise of women and children; their rise into articulate prominence, be it understood—for who is denying their right to exist? On this subject to-day only misunderstanding appears to be possible. Nevertheless, I venture my judgment that their direct admission into literature has degraded the performance by seducing writers to play to the gallery of the nurses and the nursed. And there, I think, I will drop the subject of causes. . . .

In the graphic and plastic arts innovation of any kind is for most people more conspicuous than innovation in literature: our vision preceded our minds, I suppose! Here, therefore, in the sight of all men, innovations now abound, the nature and character of which ought to be obvious. I plank down once more my conclusion that here, too, we are in the presence of infantilism, of the usual compound of the shrewd with the naïve. They tell me this and that of Marinetti, for example, but I ask if Marinetti is a child? On the contrary, he is one of the most subtle Italian spirits of the day, to whom neither Croce nor Malatesta is unknown. Distrust him, therefore, when he comes as an infant Quixote; he carries bombs, and is aware of it. (*NA*, 14, 307, 1914.)

29 Georgian Poetry (1914, 1916)

[A writer in *Poetry and Drama*] takes us back to Wordsworth and bids poets abjure 'literary' language and employ the words of every-day. What illiteracy, however, is implied in this! Back to Words-worth by all means, but *not* back to Wordsworth's failures—far more numerous than his successes, and, of course, more easily imitated. Abjure 'literary' language too, if you like; but remember that the exclusive use of 'every-day' language is equally a 'literary' affectation. I'm afraid, in fact, that these young men have not yet been entrusted by their genius with an idea to deliver. Otherwise, they would be talking of what they *must* do rather than of what they will or will not; for all good art is necessity. (*NA*, 14, 338, 1914.)

Another writer has the distressing task of examining in detail the lastest issue of the quarterly *Poetry and Drama* published from Mr. Harold Monro's Poetry Book-shop. I need only wonder what in the language's name these young versifiers are after. A recent meeting with a few of them satisfies me that they are, as they foolishly hope, remote from the world right enough, but not, as they also foolishly suppose, on any peak of Darien. Their ignorance is appalling! Not content to boast that they are not concerned with such vulgar sub-jects as politics and economics, they boast also their ignorance of the main stream of English poetry. The main stream, if you please, is not broad enough for them; it is on the little rivulets that fed it that they ply their little boats. Well, I do not deny that discoveries are to be made there—but what of them? The discoveries will be of modes and forms discovered by the great poets, worked and then abandoned. Coleridge and Wordsworth, in their retirement among the Quan-tocks, neglected neither the main stream of poetry nor the political life of their day. Regarding the first, their self-imposed task was to disestablish Pope and to crown his successor. Coleridge nominated antique glamour as the solvent of the rigidity of Pope; Wordsworth substituted the simple contemplation of nature; both, in short, were mightily concerned with their duty to their day and place. And as for the second—their interest in politics—did not Pitt employ a spy to report on their sayings and doings? Fancy Mr. Asquith apprehending danger from the whole Poetry Book-shop! (*NA*, 14, 722, 1914.)

When that I was a little little boy, Mr. Richard le Gallienne's sun was just rising upon London. Since then, it appears to me, his sun has really never set, for to the best of my belief all our minor poets derive from him in one twig or another. Mr. le Gallienne himself derived from Oscar Wilde, and Oscar Wilde from Verlaine and Flaubert and Baudelaire, and there you are—thus are the sins of the fathers continued in the children to the third and fourth generation. I flatter myself, too, that I know something of modern minor verse; my collection is perhaps the tenth best in England; and I occasionally spend an afternoon in actually re-reading it. This is a matter of duty, however, rather than of pleasure; for I conceive it to be the duty of a reader and writer to be a contemporary among contemporaries; and by no means can this be better performed than by keeping in touch with current verse. Poetry, after all, is the end by which literature is renewed from time to time. It is nearer the source of inspiration than any other form of writing. Whether, therefore, literature is to be renewed in the immediate future, and the qualities its renewal will reveal, are best discovered by a sympathetic examination of the trickles of verse that make their way into the general stream.

But the vast mass of minor poetry to-day is not in this sense original, but derivative. It is inspired, that is, not by personal experience of life, but by experiences among books. Take away the aforesaid French poets, and I doubt if there would ever have been an Oscar Wilde at all—the Oscar Wilde, at any rate, of fact. For he might very well have become a somewhat more precious John Addington Symonds or, let us say, a second-rate Pater. Similarly, but for him it is certain to my mind that Mr. le Gallienne would never have written a word. Completely without distinction of mind, lacking in intellectual energy and positively not interested in ideas, Mr. le Gallienne, but for the fatal attraction of Oscar Wilde, would, I believe, have remained where he was in Liverpool, or perhaps have risen to the provincial stage. The same literary impressionability, however, that made Mr. le Gallienne a poet when

Nature intended him for something else, has made poets of scores of young men since his day—and always, so I think, with the same outcome. They bear the marks of their literary birth as visibly as original poets carry the signs of originality in everything they do. What, for instance, are the characteristic features of the minor poets of to-day ? Not to be tedious in a small matter, I will name only two: a kind of irreverent cosmic swagger—impudent addresses and challenges to God and the like; and a habit of cynical anti-climax which they regard as the grim humour of realism. Look at almost any modern versifier you please, and I venture to say that you will find examples of one or of both these moods. Now the poet is threatening to tear God from His throne and to put himself in His place; and, in another minute, he is pulling a flower to pieces to show us the maggot at its heart. But of either or both of these moods there are certain things that we can definitely say. In the first place, it is the rarest thing in the world to find them original. I should say that not more than one man in a century is born in whom the impulse to challenge God is native and original; and as for the disposition honestly and truthfully to see the worm in every bud of beauty—men are such liars in this respect that I doubt if one is truthful about it. There are thus too many of the school to-day to allow us to suppose that they are *all* sincere. In the second place, you have only to turn to your Oscar Wilde infant school—the school of le Gallienne, Arthur Symons, etc.—to discover the literary ancestry of these characteristics. Mr. le Gallienne, in particular, had a fancy for deposing God; and all his school were affectedly cynical in the intervals of sentimentality. Lastly—I say lastly out of consideration for my readers—it can be simply stated that these particular moods, whether original or imitative, are *not* the moods of poetry.

In *Studies of Contemporary Poets*, Miss Mary C. Sturgeon makes a gallant attempt to make mountains out of molehills. She treats fifteen or so minor poets of to-day with all the seriousness with which critics would treat our fewer major poets. But they are not susceptible of it, no, not one of them! I am disposed myself to allow that Mr. W. H. Davies has written some pretty little lyrics, and that there is a puckish quality in some of Mr. James Stephens' verse that is not unpleasingly curious; but when it comes to writing an essay of interpretation about them, and still more, about poets like Mr. Lascelles Abercrombie, Mr. Rupert Brooke, Mr. Wilfrid Wilson Gibson, etc., the result is more interpretation than text.

This can be seen at once in the following extract. Miss Sturgeon is commenting upon a poem by Mr. Lascelles Abercrombie, and she asks: 'Could a great conception be stated in a simpler phrase than that of the two first lines:

> Life, the mother who lets her children play
> So seriously busy, trade and craft——?'

And she continues: 'Yet this phrase, simple and lucid as it is, conveys a sense of boundless tenderness and pity, playing over the surface of a deeper irony. Doubtless its strength and clarity come from the fact that each word is of the common coin of the daily life; but its atmosphere, an almost infinite suggestiveness of familiar things brooded over in a wistful mood, comes partly at least through the colloquial touch.'

Why, I could write as much of 'Little Boy Blue' or 'Baa-baa, black sheep.' Is it not obvious that Miss Sturgeon has read into the lines what obviously is not in them? And you may guess from this example what swans the rest of her geese become.

Only because his death has attracted public attention to his verse, a special note may be made upon Mr. Rupert Brooke. I have lately been re-reading him to discover what, perhaps, my well-known prejudice against living writers might have led me to underrate in him while he was still alive. But I confess that his somewhat pathetic death has made no difference to my judgment. Dead he is as bad a poet as he was alive. When he would express, as Miss Sturgeon says, 'sheer passion,' he becomes in my opinion merely bombastic. Listen:

> I'll break and forge the stars anew,
>   Shatter the heavens with a song;
> Immortal in my love for you,
>   Because I love you, very strong.

That may be what moderns love to call 'sheer passion,' but to my mind it contains only an affectation of passion. If I were the lady to whom the vows were being made, I should laugh and send my suitor to a newspaper office. . . . That Mr. Brooke wished to be a poet and could not arrive at it I regard as his personal tragedy. He could never forgive either himself or poetry for his failure. He had put on singing-robes in his early youth, but he found himself wearing them at a fancy-dress ball; and he was torn between

K

30 Futurism (1914)

Mr. Marinetti's Futurist Manifesto published in *The New Age* last week is, I suppose, like everything else in these pages, open to discussion. My view is that Mr. Marinetti is reviving an old quarrel that ought to have been drowned and damned by the Flood,—the quarrel of presentation with representation; and that he is on the wrong side of the controversy. The jealousy of every writer for the omnipotence of pure literature is something fanatic. As Hokusai used to hope that by the time he was a hundred and twenty every one of his drawings would be alive, every man of letters looks forward one day to writing living sentences. Absolutely no writer of any rank has ever complained, in my recollection, that his own language was not sufficient for him; but all of them have despaired of ever employing it fully. Mr. Marinetti, however, appears to assume that artists feel cramped by the common language and desire new materials of expression; and he proceeds to invent crazy typographical and onomatopœic tricks as means to this end. But as well as mistaking the despair of writers (which, as I have said, is with themselves and not with their medium), he mistakes the whole *raison d'être* of literature which is precisely not to present and reproduce, but to represent and produce. The logical mind, I maintain, has the intention of ultimately expressing in words the universe that proceeded, myth says, from a word; and our common speech is the base on which this Jacob's ladder is planted. To return now to animal sounds and typographical glyphs would be to abandon our task and to relapse into barbarism. Simplicity, lucidity, charm—these are the qualities in which our style can never be perfect enough. And Mr. Marinetti has not one of them. (*NA*, 15, 38, 1914.)

One of my colleagues observed the other day that the defect of Futurism is that it is a reaction against art not against life. It is a fine critical observation and I wish I had made it first. Hearing Messrs. Marinetti and Nevinson the other evening I was struck by their fury against their predecessors remote and of yesterday. It was to distinguish themselves from these that it appeared their campaign was being undertaken. This will never do, for to be moved by art is just not to be moved by life. I heard, too, the 'noise-tuners' at the Coliseum. The Futurists talk of representing life in place of merely reproducing life; but in fact every one of the twenty-two instruments of the orchestra reproduced some natural sound with servile fidelity. This again will never do; for if art is not the representation of life it is certainly not its reproduction. Again I remarked the emphasis laid by Messrs. Marinetti and Nevinson on the absurdity of immortality. This, I think, is the worst sign upon their movement; for an art that does not aspire to immortalize its work is vulgar from the beginning. For our mortal needs not art but contrivance is necessary and sufficient; but for the soul nothing but what at least promises to be everlasting has interest.

What perhaps is of value in Futurism is its affirmation of the claim of the age upon art. Use, it exponents say, the material of your own time for your art, for every other is more or less alien. There is something in this; but, once more, it is a question of insight. To see deeply into one's contemporary life is to see life much as it has always been and always will be. Plato writing to-day would write much the same as Plato writing two thousand five hundred years ago. The dialect of truth does not alter much. On the other hand, I agree that subjects ought to be taken from to-day. It is the treatment— above all, its depth and truth—that determines whether the resultant work is one of art. I can imagine works full of acutality and empty of art. Imagine them? Look at the bookstalls! (*NA*, 15, 181, 1914.)

Mr. Wyndham Lewis' new quarterly magazine, *Blast*, has been announced as the successor of *The Yellow Book*. But that, I imagine, is no great credit to it, for who, looking back to that period, can admit that there was any philosophy in it? Aubrey Beardsley was something of a genius, but his mind was never equal to his talents; in other words, he was a decadent genius; and who else was there of the smallest importance on *The Yellow Book*? *Blast* has the relative disadvantage of being launched without even a decadent genius to give it a symptomatic importance. It is, I find, not unintelligible—as most of the reviewers will doubtless say —but not worth the understanding. . . .

What, from this point of view, is its significance? My answer is that it is another sign of the spiritual anarchism of modern society. This, believe me, is not cant on my part. I am old enough to have lived through the *Yellow Book* period from its start and to have shared in every phase since, both in what may be called their practice as well as their theories. Without boasting, I can say I have known them all. And the conclusion left in my mind is that for the last thirty years the spiritual character of our intellectuals has been declining. To what we must look for a renaissance I have often tried to say in these notes; but I can see now, from the appearance of *Blast* and from the number and quality of its probable victims, that *The New Age* must be more definite than ever in the future. To tell the truth, the work is at present incredibly difficult. Even to think straight in these days requires an effort; as the alienist often finds it hard to preserve his sanity among his patients. (*NA*, 15, 229, 1914.)

When I wrote my note on *Blast* last week I had not read Mr. Wyndham Lewis' chief contribution—'Enemy of the Stars.' It deserves to be called an extraordinary piece of work much more than Miss Rebecca West's study of 'Indissoluble Matrimony.' The latter has all the vices of the *Blast* school, excessive and barbaric ornamentation, violent obscurity, degraded imagery; but unmixed with any idea. 'Enemy of the Stars,' on the other hand, contains ideas of an almost grandiose dimension, though felt rather than thought. This, indeed, I take to be the characteristic of the school—that they prefer the feeling of ideas to the clearly thinking of them. Doubtless this preference has been growing upon our young men lately, as a reaction from the dry light of rationalism. Doubtless also it will provide in the end fresh material for reason to elucidate. But for the present the movement appears to me to be the very devil. Brilliant common sense, which we of *The New Age* have taken as our watchword, is obviously in peril from the neo-mysticism; so, too, I fear, is reason itself. I'm afraid, however, that the plunge into the dark is going to be seductive of the young. It sounds romantic, it makes a great clatter both in the mind and in the world, it stirs the solar plexus, and it produces the illusion of life. All the same, it is past racial history; and the time-spirit will be revenged on such as stir its bones. I will return to the subject if nobody else deals with it. (*NA*, 15, 253, 1914.)

Perhaps I am becoming a little sympathetic in my new age. The second issue of *Blast* appears to me much better than the first. Except for that Balkan fragment, the 'Enemy of the Stars,' by Mr. Wyndham Lewis, the first number of *Blast* contained nothing of literature that was even interesting. The present issue—largely, I suppose, because Mr. Lewis is the main contributor—contains a good deal. In fact, it is worth buying and reading. Vorticism, which, until yesterday, was an enigma to me, has now become, I will not say intelligible, but intelligent. And, as sure as I am alive, even Mr. Pound's Imagism, which only last week was an American Sphinx in my mind—a hybrid, that is, between the commonplace and the incomprehensible—has begun to shape itself into a familiar form. Mr. Lewis, I need not say, can write; and when he chooses he can even make himself understood. Quite a change in this respect has come over his attitude in the interval between two *Blasts*. In the first he was designedly obscure, leading one to suspect he had nothing to conceal. Vorticism was then not only the last word in Art but the first that had ever been uttered. Its mission was to reduce the past and its contemporaries to oblivious ages. In the current issue, however, Mr. Lewis obliges us by explaining himself;

and, after all, it turns out that he had really something to say, which he now says. But Vorticism is no longer, except in isolated paragraphs that have failed to be deleted, the only form that Art is permitted to take; it pleads for admission as *one* form. This changed attitude I personally find more ingratiating than the old monomania; in which there was something Judaic. You see, it has changed mine!

Let me first copy out a few sentences from Mr. Lewis' contributions. Note, in the first place, that Mr. Lewis shares *The New Age*'s detestation of the Naturalistic or Realist school. He says: 'Imitation, an inherently unselective registering of impressions, is an absurdity.' 'The first reason for not imitating Nature is that you cannot convey the emotion you receive at the contact of Nature by imitating her, but only by becoming her.' I think we have made that criticism ourselves many times; and also the suggestion that follows. 'The finest artists,' says Mr. Lewis, 'are those men who are so trained and sensitized [a horrid word, by the way!] that they have a perpetually renewed power of *doing what nature does*.' And again: 'If the material world were not empirical and matter simply for science, but were organized as in the imagination, we should live as though we were dreaming.' Applying all this to Vorticism—both the criticism and the doctrine—it can be seen now *why* the Vorticists first repudiated so much of past and current Art: they repudiated its naturalism, that is, its imitation of nature. On the other hand, they proceeded to attempt to plunge into the 'vortices' of Nature's forces, where these are still primitive, potential and on their way to manifestation (see 'The Enemy of the Stars'); and to direct them into forms which unaided nature would probably never have achieved. Hence Vorticist pictures; forms never yet seen in nature, but made of the stuff of which natural forms are made; determined by the same natural energy, but directed by artistic intelligence instead of by nature. If, without irony or blasphemy, we suppose Mr. Lewis, instead of God, to have been the 'Spirit of Nature,' the world would have become manifest as the Vorticists now represent it. A queer world, you may say; but doubtless we should have got used to it as we have to God's world!

I flatter myself that Mr. Lewis will be pleased at my comprehension so far. But now for a step farther. Theoretically, as I have said before, the number of possible worlds is infinite. 'The infinite is infinite in an infinite number of ways.' In the *Mahabharata*, for example, you may read of hosts of non-human orders of intelligence existing contemporaneously with our own race and seldom or never coming into any contact with us. As well as these, the *potential* variations are endless. Monsters, in our eyes, could conceivably be created as readily as new forms of flowers. Mr. Wells once wrote a 'Vorticist' work, *The Island of Dr. Moreau*, in which he actually imagined them. And Mr. Shaw has talked airily of a 'super-snake.' The repulsion I feel, however, towards all these is the reflection (at least, I hope so) of the repulsion the spirit of *our* world itself feels. I refuse to be interested, except in hostility, in anything that nature *could* do if she wished; and confine my friendly interest to discovering what nature actually *does* wish yet cannot do. Mr. Lewis, if I understand him, claims the right to manipulate the plastic forces of nature and to make a world of his own out of them. I do not deny that it is possible; what I deny is that it is right. The circumscription —the Ring Pass-Not—that nature has put upon herself is a circumscription that the artist should cheerfully accept; his business, it appears to me, is to forward nature by divining her plans and manifesting what is in her mind, not to use her energies for confusing and frustrating her intentions. J'accuse Mr. Lewis of being, to the best of his ability, disloyal to nature. We agree that nature should not be imitated. The second commandment must be obeyed in art as well as in ethics. But we are hopelessly at variance when the next step is to be taken. Mr. Lewis is for creating a 'nature' of his own imagination. I am for perfecting the nature that already exists in strenuous imperfection. He is for Vorticism; I am for the idealization of the actual. It is worth quarrelling about. . . .

Mr. Pound's Imagism is not Vorticist, whatever else it may be. His new volume of verse, *Cathay*, is excellent. The translations from the Chinese are a revelation. (*NA*, 17, 309, 1915.)

32 Ezra Pound (1915, 1917, 1918, 1921)

As Mr. James Douglas has half accused *The New Age* of inventing Mr. Ezra Pound, I may perhaps spend with profit a little critical subtlety in disproving it. However often we may have mentioned Mr. Pound's name, it is at least certain that we have never countenanced his theories. But then Mr. Pound is so much better than his theories that to dispose of them is by no means to dispose of him. What, in fact, he does in the company his theories keep, it is hard to say; for they do not distinguish him, but link him with inferior schools; they do not influence his work, except when he is wilful like an American child; and they afford him no help. I would part Mr. Pound from his theories as often as I found him clinging to one, for they will in the end be his ruin.

Cathay, as I said last week, contains some excellent work. If I were to say that it contains the best and even the only good work Mr. Pound has yet done, my judgment might be defended. The volume contains, among other poems, a re-print of 'The Seafarer,' Mr. Pound's masterly translation from the original Anglo-Saxon. This poem, which *The New Age* had the honour of first publishing, is without doubt one of the finest literary works of art produced in England during the last ten years. . . . Mr. Pound will not, I hope, mind me quoting two of his Chinese translations with the invitation to my readers to compare them with 'The Seafarer.' [Quotes 'Song of the Bowmen of Shu' and 'The River Merchant's Wife: A Letter.']

Now nobody, I think, whatever his prejudices against free rhythm (and I share them), would deny that these two, let us call them compositions, are compositions of art. Both are, it is true, so simple as to be almost natural; they might, that is, be *almost* records of actuality and nothing more. And both, from a superficial view, are naïve and artless. But looked at carefully and reflected upon, they will be seen to be full of artifice and quite as unlike anything actual as they are also like. The line between their 'realism' and their art is, in fact, difficult to indicate; yet it most certainly can be felt. After all, Rihaku was *not* a Merchant's Wife, nor was Kutsugen a bowman of Shu. Both were artists sympathetically delighting in the re-creation and perfectioning of the natural. Our pleasure in them is therefore that of art and not of nature. Indeed, it would be improper to take pleasure in the compositions if they were authentically personal. Only the fact that we can assure ourselves that the incidents for the writer are imaginary; or, at any rate, that their narration is a pleasure to him; permits us to set aside the moral discomfort that would surely be felt if they were real, and to enjoy the pure pleasure of their art. They are thus reality raised by art to sublimity: the natural perfected, and hence robbed of its 'moral' obligations.

I would make two further observations. As in 'The Seafarer,' the thoughts contained in the Chinese poems are of a very simple character. The imaginary persons are without subtlety and almost, you might say, without mind. But it cannot be the case that only simple natures can be the subjects of poetry; or that 'naturalness' belongs to them alone. I have noted in the free-rhythmists a tendency to confine themselves to the elementary emotions of elementary people; as if the possession of a cultivated mind excluded its owner from poetry. But Browning, I suggest, was quite as simple, straight-forward and 'natural' in, say, 'Bishop Bloughram's Apology,' as Rihaku was in his Merchant's Wife's Letter. The difference is that Browning was 'perfecting' the expression of a powerful and subtle mind, while Rihaku was perfecting the mind relatively of a child. The extension of the directness and simplicity, the veracity and the actuality aimed at by free-rhythmists, into subtler regions than the commonplace is advisable if they are not to keep in the nursery of art. My other observation is on the subject of the form. I have not denied being 'pleased' with the poems I have quoted, though their form is that of free-rhythm. Nobody, as I said, can fail indeed to derive some pleasure from them. At the same time the pleasure is much less than I should derive from the same contents in an orderly form. Content is not everything in poetry, as everybody knows. As well as the content the form itself is an integral and, in great poetry, an indistinguishable element of the pleasure. The form and the content are at once one and two. In these poems, however, as in all free-rhythm, the form is not a positive source of pleasure, though I admit that it is not a subtraction from the pleasure. It is simply absent. But given a content as pure (that is, as perfectly natural) and a form equally *perfectly* natural—that is, delicately regularized, selected, artistic—the total pleasure must obviously be more intense. From an unaccompanied melody we should rise to a symphony. This, it will be seen, does not condemn free-rhythm, except as an imperfect form of art. It is, in fact, a transitional form between no poetry at all or a pedantic poetry, and perfect poetry. As a phenomenon of our time it is, in part, due to writers who simply have no poetry in them and, in part, to writers genuinely reacting against the school of Tennyson: the revolutionaries and the charlatans once more mingling as in every reform movement. To which of these component parties in the school of free-rhythm Mr. Pound belongs there is, of course, no doubt. And hence I wish him speedily out of it. (*NA*, 17, 332–3, 1915.)

Free rhythm, in my sense of the word, is one of the liberties of the kingdom of poetry which itself is essentially formal beauty. It does not imply freedom *from* regular or formal rhythm, but merely freedom *within* it. Let the vers librettists compare the free rhythm of Shakespeare within the limits of blank verse with the freedom of their own school outside all formal limits—not even Miss Lowell, I believe, will claim to be more free of poetry. (*NA*, 20, 255, 1917.)

Under the title of *Ezra Pound: His Metric and Poetry*, a whole book —really, however, only an essay—has been devoted to the work of our well-known contributor and sometime pièce de resistance. For this honour, if honour it be, I think that Mr. Pound is indebted more to what he has preached than to what he has practised; for on his actual achievement, considerable though it is, I doubt whether even in America anybody could have been found to write a book about his work. Mr. Pound, however, will not deny that he is an American in this respect, if in none other, that he always likes to hitch his waggon to a star. He has always a ton of precept for a pound of example. And in America, more than in any other country save, perhaps, Germany, it appears to be required of a man that there shall be 'significance,' intention, aim, theory—anything you like expressive of direction—in everything he does. As I have before pointed out, there does not appear to me to be anything *very* original in the creation of poetic images, or even in the employment of irregular metric; neither of them can be said to constitute a new departure in poetic technique. Yet, as we have seen, Mr. Pound has elevated each of them to be the star of a cult, with the consequence that we now have professed 'schools' of poetry calling themselves Imagist or Verslibrist respectively. . . .

It must be admitted, however, that this habit of Mr. Pound has its good as well as its somewhat absurd side; there is only a step, you know, from the ridiculous to the sublime. It must also be affirmed, however it may reflect upon our English critics, that it is precisely the good side of Mr. Pound's technique which they usually condemn. For the good side consists in this, that all the poets who can claim to belong to the school of Mr. Pound must display in addition to the above-mentioned defects, the certain and positive merits of study of their art, and deliberate craftsmanship. No poet, I think, dare claim to be a pupil of Mr. Pound who cannot prove that he has been to school to poetry and submitted himself to a craft-apprenticeship; and no poet will long command Mr. Pound's approval who is not always learning and experimenting. Now this, which I call the good side in Mr. Pound's doctrine, is disliked in England, where it has for years been the habit of critics to pretend that poetry grows on bushes or in parsley-beds. That poetry should be the practice of 'a learned, self-conscious craft' to be carried on by a 'guild of adepts' appears to Mr. Archer, for example, to be a heresy of the first order. How much of the best poetry, he exclaims, has been written with 'little technical study behind it'; and how little necessary, therefore, any previous learning is. To the dogs with Mr. Pound's doctine! Let the motto over the gates of the Temple of Poetry be: 'No previous experience required.' It will be seen, of course, how the confusion in Mr. Archer's mind has arisen. Because it is a fact that the 'best' poetry *looks* effortless, he has fallen into the spectator's error of concluding that it *is* effortless. And because, again, a considerable part of the work of the 'learned, self-conscious craftsmen' is pedantic and artificial, he has been confirmed in his error. The truth of the matter, however, is with Mr. Pound. Dangerous as it may be to require that a poet shall be learned in his profession, it is much more dangerous to depreciate his learning. By a happy fluke, it may be, a perfect poem may occasionally be written 'without previous study'; from too much previous study there may also occasionally result only verse smelling of the lamp; but in the long run and for the cultivation of poetry as an art there is no doubt that the most fruitful way is the way of the craftsman and the adept. (*NA*, 23, 201, 1918.)

Mr. Ezra Pound has recently gone abroad, perhaps for one year, perhaps for two, perhaps for good. Following the old and, in my opinion, the bad example first set by a man of letters, Landor, Mr. Pound has shaken the dust of London from his feet with not too emphatic a gesture of disgust, but, at least, without gratitude to this country. I can perfectly well understand, even if I find it difficult to approve. Mr. Pound has been an exhilarating influence for culture in England; he has left his mark upon more than one of the arts, upon literature, music, poetry and sculpture; and quite a number of men and movements owe their initiation to his self-sacrificing stimulus; among them being relatively popular successes as well as failures. With all this, however, Mr. Pound, like so many others who have striven for the advancement of intelligence and culture in England, has made more enemies than friends, and far more powerful enemies than friends. Much of the Press has been deliberately closed by cabal to him; his books have for some time been ignored or written down; and he himself has been compelled to live on much less than would support a navvy. His fate, as I have said, is not unusual: I could parallel it near home and with more than one instance. Taken by and large, England hates men of culture until they are dead. But, all the same, it is here or nowhere that the most advanced trenches of the spirit are to be found; and it is here, I believe, that the enemy will have to be defeated. Mr. Pound has gone, I understand, to France; he is certain sooner or later to find himself in Paris; where the apparent ease of the work of intelligence has flattered many a man of letters that he was contributing to the progress of mankind. A delusion and an illusion! For, in fact, France has long ceased to be in the van of culture and is now, in my judgment, scarcely bringing up the straggling rear. Even with Mr. Pound in it, I expect nothing from Paris for the next quarter of a century. . . .

Before leaving England, Mr. Pound was generous enough to draw up for publication his intellectual will and testament. On the preceding page is printed, in the form of Axiomata, Mr. Pound's credo, his summary conclusions concerning the nature of the world. I shall leave to my readers the pleasant task of interpreting Mr. Pound's 'Axiomata' in terms of life and art, but only after remarking on what appears to me to be the kernel of Mr. Pound's creed—its opening article that 'the intimate essence of the universe is *not* of the same nature as our own consciousness.' Everything else, I think, both in the Creed and in Mr. Pound's work, past, present and future, is implicitly contained in this affirmation, and the more certainly so from the fact that it is at once Mr. Pound's most comprehensive, fundamental and decisive statement. Taking it as the basis of Mr. Pound's Creed, what is to be remarked in it? In the first place, that it is a negative statement, a denial, the reactionary and counter-assertion of a corresponding positive; and, secondly, that the 'consciousness' implied in the phrase 'our own consciousness,' is confined in effect to self-consciousness, waking consciousness, in short, to our normal everyday rational consciousness. But the presence of these elements in the first article of Mr. Pound's Creed is not insignificant; and the evidence is abundant when we transfer our attention from his creed to his work. Writing as a professed literary judge, I should always have said; indeed, I have often said—that the two most serious defects in Mr. Pound's work have been and are his enmity to religion and his lack of psychological depth. The one has introduced a bizarre atheistic or rationalistic *mannerism* into his style; and the other is responsible for much of his pre-occupation with the *trivialities* of art-forms—studio-talk, as I have called it. The cat is out of the bag for everybody, even without literary judgment, to see for himself now; there it is stalking abroad in the full light of Mr. Pound's explicit article. Mr. Pound's attitude towards religion (or the world of potentialities—since it is clear that *if* we are not of the same stuff as the 'universe,' the limits of possible knowledge are defined by the actual)—is actively negative, unsympathetic and hostile; and his expectation of 'consciousness' is confined to what may emerge from the self-consciousness alone. Paris, under these circumstances, has nothing to teach and nothing to learn. (*NA*, 28, 126–7, 1921.)

[Concluding a review of Pound's *Gaudier-Brzeska*:] A critique of Brzeska, and of Epstein, whose work is greater, is yet to be done. All our writers upon art have hitherto ignominiously failed to make it; and Mr. Pound first and worst among them. Some day, perhaps, a critic of the artists' own level will arise. Meanwhile Brzeska has gone to his death in France un-understood, and Mr. Epstein is at the disposal of a military tribunal composed of tradesmen. (*NA*, 19, 182, 1916. When this passage was written, Epstein was finding it unaccountably difficult to have his induction delayed so that he might complete several major works and thereby pay his debts. It was not unusual for delays to be granted in such circumstances.)

The art-critic of *The Times* having remarked that 'the public hardly looks at the sculpture in the Academy, or outside it,' Mr. John Tweed, an eminent sculptor himself, has now uttered a public lamentation in agreement with him. Sculpture to-day, he says, is an art without an audience; and he quotes a Belgian artist who told him what heroes our contemporary sculptors in this country must be to continue their work in the face of a unanimous neglect. I am not so sure, however, that the sculptors of to-day do not thoroughly well deserve the fate to which they now find themselves condemned. In the economy of the arts, or, if you prefer the phrase, in the strategy of æsthetics, nothing is more necessary from time to time in each of the arts than an iconoclast—by which, of course, I by no means wish to indicate a destroyer simply, but rather a creator of new forms. Such a pioneer is of necessity a little rude to his immediate predecessors and to such of his contemporaries as are sheep. But in the end, nevertheless, if they will only accept and recognize him, he will revive their art for them. In the case of sculpture, however, the two such iconoclasts as have recently appeared—Mr. Epstein and the late Gaudier-Brzeska—were instantly set upon, not by the public, but by their contemporaries, and walled within a neglect far more complete than the neglect sculpture in general has received. Just when it appeared that they might be about to re-awaken public interest in carven forms, the rest of the sculptors hurried to silence them, with the consequence that at this moment there is literally nobody engaged in sculpture in whom the intelligent public takes the smallest interest. As sculptors have treated sculpture, so the public now treats sculptors. (*NA*, 23, 74, 1918.)

34 T. E. Hulme and T. S. Eliot (1920, 1921)

Our late colleague and common friend, Lieut. T. E. Hulme (as he was when he was killed on active service) has left, it appears, a quantity of MSS., chiefly in the form of notes, amounting in the whole to several books, I should say. The question of their editorship and publication is still unsettled, though I am not without hope that another of our old mutual friends, Mr. F. S. Flint, may be persuaded to undertake the labour of delight. In the meanwhile, having been privileged to look over the MSS., I may offer my opinion that in T. E. Hulme our nation lost as promising a mind as we had amongst us, which is to say a great deal in view of the actual losses the world knows it has sustained. Hulme's mind was constructed on the grand scale simple, and the impression irresistibly formed of him by everybody capable of judgment was one of capacity. It is obvious, too, from the material left by him that his conception of his life's work was proportionate to his abilities. He was still very young, but the fragments he had begun to accumulate were plainly intended for a cyclopean architecture. None of us, I am sure, had any adequate idea of the industry with which Hulme was preparing himself for a long and great career. In personal contact he appeared to be too overflowing with energy and bonhomie to be capable, as yet, of the sustained study and practice indispensable to great expression; but there is the evidence of the rick of MSS. which I have seen to prove that all the while Hulme was gathering himself and his powers for the work he intended one day to accomplish. (*NA*, 27, 259, 1920.)

A very serious critic of our day is Mr. T. S. Eliot; and I commend his essays wherever they are to be found. Of American birth and Harvard education, he has made himself a good European; and in all matters concerning literature his judgment is both wide and weighty. If I may say so, he delivers his judgment with rather too detached an

L

air, as if he were a High Court judge adjudicating fully and impartially but over a question of no emotional concern to himself; but, on the other hand, the feeling is only concealed; if the reader will watch his own reactions, it is not absent. The truth appears to be that Mr. Eliot cultivates expressionlessness as other people cultivate expression. He would not have you suspect that the matters in hand are of great emotional concern to him. They should be, he suggests, of great emotional concern to his readers; but for himself he prefers to appear to be above that plane. *He* can keep cool where the rest *ought* to be enthusiastic; but at bottom, as I have said, he is really more enthusiastic than most of his readers are ever likely to be. And that is his real complaint against them; and the origin of his mask. 'No,' he seems to say to himself, 'I will not let my readers think that I am more concerned than they are. If they are cold, I will appear colder. My heart shall not betray me—at least, in advance of theirs.' The result is a curious atmosphere unique in modern literature: a style at once lawyerlike and romantic, and a judgment at once intimate and distant. It is a phenomenon worth attention, one of the current 'events' of literary criticism; and once more I commend Mr. Eliot's essays to my readers' notice. (*NA*, 28, 259, 1921.)

35 The Avant-garde: 'Making no compromise with the public taste' (1918)

I have lately had sent me the recent issues of an American magazine of belles-lettres, to which reference has been made before in these columns—*The Little Review*. Mr. Ezra Pound has for some months been the 'foreign' or exile editor of it; and I gather from the nature of the contributions that he has practically commandeered most of the space of the recent issues. A series of letters and some stories by Mr. Wyndham Lewis; letters, stories and verse by Mr. Pound; ditto, ditto, ditto by other—shall I say London?—writers—are evidence that Mr. Pound's office is no sinecure. He delivers the goods. The aim of *The Little Review*, as defined without the least attempt at camouflage by the editress (that is to say, the real American director of the venture) is to publish articles, stories, verses and drawings of pure art—whatever that may be. It is not demanded of them that they shall be true—or false; that they shall have a meaning —single or double; that they shall be concerned with life—or fancy. Nothing, in fact, is asked of them but that they shall be art, just art. Less explicitly, but to the same effect, both Mr. Pound and Mr. Wyndham Lewis subscribe to the same formula. They, too, are after art, nothing but art. But in some respects they define themselves more clearly. From Mr. Wyndham Lewis, for instance, I gather that the aim of *The Little Review* artists is to differentiate themselves from the mob. Art would seem to consist, indeed, in this differentiation or self-separation. Whatever puts a gulf between yourself and the herd, and thus 'distinguishes' you, is, and must be, art, because of this very effect. And Mr. Pound carries on the doctrine a stage by insisting that the only thing that matters about the mob is to deliver individuals from it. Art, in short, is the discovery, maintenance and culture of individuals. . . .

Read Mr. Lewis' letters, for example, in the issues of *The Little Review* here under notice. The writer is obviously a very clever man, with a good experience and judgment of life, and possessed of a powerful style. But he has chosen to exhibit himself as a clever gymnast of words, with innumerable finnicking fancies against taking this or that lest he should be confused with the 'mob.' And Mr. Pound is in much the same state. What is the need of it, I ask, in their case? Unlike most of the other writers (I specially except Mr. T. S. Eliot, whose poem the 'Hippopotamus' is impressive), neither Mr. Lewis nor Mr. Pound has any need to 'cultivate' an individuality, or to surround it with walls and moats of poses. Neither has any need whatever to appear clever in order to be clever. On the contrary, both of them have need to do exactly the reverse—namely, to cut their too exuberant individuality down to the quick, and to reveal their cleverness by concealing it. Simplicity, as Oscar Wilde said—he, of course, only said it, he never really thought it—is the last refuge of complexity. And I put it to Mr. Lewis and Mr. Pound that with just a little more individuality and with just a little more cleverness their ambition will be to be indistinguishable from the mob either by their individuality or their cleverness. They will not succeed in this, of course. Individuality and cleverness, like murder, will out. The aim, however, of the wise possessor of either is to conceal it in subtler and subtler forms of common sense and simplicity. (*NA*, 22, 332, 1918.)

From the recent issues of *The Little Review*, a monthly magazine published in America under the foreign editorship of Mr. Ezra Pound and the American editorship of Miss Anderson (it always, by the way, takes a number of people to edit a little review), I see what I must have missed before—the characteristic sub-title of the magazine: 'Making no compromise with the public taste.' Already it is to compromise with public taste to deny it; indeed, nothing is more compromising than to be found in explicit negation with public taste. The thing itself and the negation of it are as closely related as the poles. But apart from this, how of the coterie the phrase smells, how very little indeed is the area taken under review. For myself, as I have often observed, what is good enough for the classics is good enough for me; and since their habit has invariably been to write about what interests everybody in language that everybody understands, the nearer we approach to public taste the better is our style.

The Little Review will have to pay, however, for its contempt of the classic aim; and not alone in finding itself neglected. Neglect, on the whole, means nothing very much; success is a matter of time for everything that is really classic. On the other hand, deliberately to incur neglect by writing for the few involves the further risk of more and more deserving it. I mean to say that whoever makes a boast of writing for a coterie sooner or later finds himself writing for a coterie of a coterie, and at last for himself alone. It cannot be otherwise. As the progress of the classic is from the one to the many, the progress of the romantic is from the many to the one; and the more sincerely the latter is a romantic, the sooner he arrives at his journey's end. The involution of aim thus brought about is obvious already in the succession of works of the chief writers of *The Little Review*. They grow cleverer and cleverer, and, at the same time, more and more unintelligible to the public—including myself. I am staggered by the cleverness of such a writer as Mr. Wyndham Lewis; and a little more so by the cleverness of Mr. James Joyce. But in the case of both of them, I find myself growing more and more annoyingly mystified, bewildered and repelled. Is it, I ask, that they do not write for readers like me? Then their circle must be contracting, for I am one of many who used to read them with pleasure. And who are they gaining while losing us? Are their new readers more intensive if fewer, and better worth while for their quality than we were for our numbers? But I am not going to allow the favourable answers. The fact is that the writers of *The Little Review* are getting too clever even for coterie, and will soon be read only by each other . . . or themselves.

A characteristic example of what I mean is to be found in the opening chapter of Mr. James Joyce's new novel, *Ulysses*, of which a long instalment appears in the issue of *The Little Review* for March. This is how it begins:—

> Stately, plump Buck Mulligan came from the stairway, bearing a bowl of lather on which a mirror and a razor lay crossed. A yellow dressing-gown, ungirdled, was sustained gently behind him on the mild morning air. He held the bowl aloft and intoned. . . .

Now it is clear that such a passage has not been written without a great deal of thought; and if thought were art, it might be called an artistic passage. But, on the contrary, thought is not only not art, but the aim of art is to conceal thought. In perfection, indeed, art is indistinguishable from nature. The obvious thoughtfulness of the passage I have quoted is, therefore, an objection to it; and the more so since it provokes an inspection it is unable to sustain. Challenged to 'think' about what the writer is saying, the reader at once discovers that the passage will not bear thinking about. He asks, for instance, *whence* Buck Mulligan came from the staircase; *how* he managed to balance a crossed mirror and razor on a bowl's edge—and, particularly, while bearing them aloft; and what mild air it was that sustained the tails of a man's dressing-gown. To these questions deliberately provoked by the obvious care of the writer there is either no answer or none forthcoming without more thought than the detail is worth. The passage, in short, suffers from being aimed at a diminishing coterie; and it succeeds in satisfying, I imagine, only the writer of it who is alone in all its secrets. Mr. James Joyce had, I think, the makings of a great writer—not a popular writer, but a classic writer. To become what he was he needed to be opened out, to be simplified, to conceal his cleverness, to write more and more for the world. In *The New Age*, I believe, he would have been set to writing reviews for a year or two—in other words, to trying to see things as the world will one day see them. But first in *The Egoist* and now in *The Little Review* he has been directed to cultivate his faults, his limitations, his swaddling clothes of genius, with the result I have described that he is in imminent danger of brilliant provincialism.

Mr. Ezra Pound, for all his unabated enthusiasm, is not a severe enough coryphæus to be safely entrusted with the education of genius. He is indiscriminating in his praise as well as in his censure. Milton, we know, he dismisses without a qualification—a sufficient example of his massive recklessness. But, on the other hand, Mr. Wyndham Lewis and Mr. James Joyce are simply 'it,' and equally without qualification. Were this attitude consistent even, it might be less unamusing; but, alas, Mr. Pound has himself qualms and misgivings that lead us to suspect that his Jove is often nodding. Let us take Mr. Pound's own essays in *The Little Review*, the chief of which is a commentated anthology, very well done (for the second time), of modern French poets. He begins in his absolute fashion by declaring that it is a disgrace to know no language beside your own; and America, in particular, is warned that its intellectual affairs 'cannot be conducted on a monolingual [unilingual?] basis.' Very well, but in a minute or two we have Mr. Pound's confession that he 'cannot take much interest in the problem of the mute "e" in French verse.' Such like technicalities in a foreign tongue, he goes on, 'cannot have for us the importance they have to a man writing in that tongue.' Which is to say, I suggest, that, after all, America's affairs of culture will need to be conducted on a unilingual basis, since even so good a French scholar as Mr. Ezra Pound can take no interest in what is the A B C of French culture. Truth to tell, the cult of French verse by an English critic is in nine cases out of ten an affectation admired in England, perhaps, but secretly smiled at in Paris. I have sat with French writers in Paris, in fact, and heard them politely patronizing the efforts of well-known English Gallophils to criticize French verse. If Mr. Pound could hear them en famille, I doubt whether he would invite America to share his experience. (*NA*, 23, 89, 1918.)

Just when we in Europe were beginning to envy America her promise, contrasting it with the winter of our own discontent, 'the authorities' (as one might say the furies, the parcæ or the weird sisters) have descended upon our unfortunate but deserving friend, *The Little Review*, and suspended its mail service on account of its publication of a chapter of Mr. James Joyce's new novel, *Ulysses*. That such an absurd act of puritanic spleen should be possible after and before years of world-war is evidence that, after all, spiritual meanness is hard to transcend; and it confirms the justice or, at least, the apprehension expressed in Mr. Ezra Pound's bon mot that the U.S.A. should be renamed the Y.M.C.A. Not only is *The Little Review* perfectly harmless; would to heaven, indeed, that it were or could be otherwise, for never can any good be done by something incapable of doing harm; but the *Ulysses* of Mr. James Joyce is one of the most interesting literary symptoms in the whole literary world, and its publication is very nearly a public obligation. Such sincerity, such energy, such fearlessness as Mr. Joyce's are rare in any epoch, and most of all in our own; and on that very account they demand to be given at least the freedom of the press. What the giant American can *fear* from Mr. Joyce or from his publication in *The Little Review* passes understanding. Abounding in every variety of crime and stupidity as America is, even if *Ulysses* were a literary crime committed in a journal of the largest circulation, one more or less could not make much difference to America. But *Ulysses* is, of course, no crime; but, on the contrary, a noble experiment; and its suppression will, in consequence, sadden the virtuous at the same time that it gratifies the base. America, we may say, is not going to 'get culture' by stamping upon every germ of new life. America's present degree of cultural toleration may ensure a herb-garden, but not a flower will grow upon the soil of Comstock. It only remains for some reputable English publisher to produce

Ulysses to secure a notable triumph for the Empire over America.

Among the scores of interesting experiments in composition and style exhibited in *Ulysses*, not the least novel is Mr. Joyce's attempt to develop a theory of harmonies in language. By compounding nouns with adjectives or adjectives with adverbs, Mr. Joyce tries to convey to the reader a complex of qualities or ideas simultaneously instead of successively. 'Eglingtoneyes looked up skybrightly.' In such a sentence agglutination has been carried beyond the ordinary level of particles into the plane of words; and the effect is, as Miss Evelyn Scott points out in *The Dial*, to present a multitude of images as if they were one. Thus 'a new and complex knowledge of self' finds its 'appropriate medium of expression in terms of art.' I am not so sure that Mr. Joyce has not carried the experiment too far; but this, again, is a virtue rather than a defect in a pioneer. Moreover, as I have often said, the world needs a few studio-magazines like *The Little Review* and a few studio-writers like Mr. James Joyce. What does it matter if, in his enthusiasm, Mr. Joyce travels beyond the limits of good taste, beyond, that is to say, the already cultivated? If only a single new literary convention is thereby brought into common use, his work will have been done. More than ever, in view of the example of experiment just mentioned, the immediate publication of *Ulysses* in England is imperative; and every literary craftsman in the country should make a point of insisting upon it. (*NA*, 28, 306–7.)

The English Language

'Language,' Orage writes in the first of the following selections, 'is not a product of logic and science, but of art and taste.' His opposition to changes in orthography and to prescriptive conceptions of grammar and pronunciation resulted from his belief that experience and culture find their most complete embodiment in language. In the importance he attaches to it, evident both in this section and in 'Discriminations,' Orage is in accord with contemporary thought. His sense of the difference between individual concrete expression and linguistic universals, formalized by his contemporary Saussure as that between '*parole*' and '*langue*,' was intuitive; the former he connected with pronunciation. For his discussion of the relationship between oral and printed literature, see 'The Literary Kinds.'

36 Spelling, Pronunciation, and Dialect (1918, 1913, 1914)

The Simplified Spelling Society has broken loose from obscurity again in the issue of a new pamphlet called *Breaking the Spell: an Appeal to Common Sense*. A preface contributed by Dr. Macan rehearses all the old 'reasons' for simplifying our spelling with as little attention as ever to the real reasons against it. 'Spelling,' we are told, 'should be the simplest of all arts.' It is so in Spanish, in Italian, in Welsh and in Dutch; and it was so in Greek and Latin. Why not, therefore, in English? The reasoning, however, is ridiculous, for it assumes that it was by some deliberate and self-conscious design that these languages came to be spelled phonetically, and, hence, that we have only to follow them enough (and the advice of the S.S.S.) in order to place our language in a similar state. Language, however, is not a product of logic and science, but of art and taste. It is determined, in consequence, not by reason alone, but by the totality of our judgment in which many other factors than reason are included. To ask us to 'reform' our spelling in order to make it 'reasonable' is to ask us to forgo the satisfaction of every intellectual taste save that of logic: a procedure that would not only 'reform' our spelling, but all literature into the bargain. It is pretended that the adoption of simplified spelling would have, at worst, only a passing effect upon the well-being of literature. If, for example, all the English classics were re-spelled in conformity with phonetic rules, and their use made general, very soon, we are told, we should forget their original idiosyncracies, and love them in their new spelling as much as ever. I can only imagine that people who argue in this way have been blinded in their taste in their pursuit of rationalistic uniformity. Literature employs words not for their rational meaning alone, not even for their sound alone, but for their combined qualities of meaning, sound, *sight*, association, history, and a score of other attributes. By reducing words to a rational rule of phonetic spelling, more than half of these qualities would be entirely, or almost entirely, eliminated. A re-spelled Shakespeare, for instance, if it should ever take the place of the present edition, would be a new Shakespeare—a Shakespeare translated from the coloured language in which he thought and wrote into a language of logical symbols. An exact analogy—as far as any analogy can be exact—for the proposal of the S.S.S. would be to propose to abolish the use of colour in pictorial art, and to produce everything in black and white. The colour-blind would, no doubt, be satisfied in the one case; and, in the other, the word-blind would be equally pleased. Fortunately, both proposals have the same chance of success. (*NA*, 23, 334, 1918.)

The efforts of Professor Walter Rippman to reduce the pronunciation of English to a system of phonetics are now supported by an equally mechanical notion, that of fixing the standard pronunciation and embodying its records on the phonograph. The idea, unfortunately, is as practicable as the collection in their museums and zoological gardens of pinned and living creatures; for there is nothing to prevent anybody preserving the record of his own voice and nobody to dissuade him from thinking his pronunciation standard. On the other hand, what its author (Mr. Benjamin Dunville) will never obtain is a record of the really standard living pronunciation of English. This is as much a matter of life as the flying of birds, which not the most realistic aviary can reproduce. The pronunciation of even the most 'correct' of us varies as greatly as every other mode of expression with the circumstances in which we find ourselves. The standard, in short, can only be uttered and heard when the conditions are happy—and these are scarcely likely to be provided when Mr. Dunville and his phonograph are about. For what my protest is worth, I protest with all my soul against the threatened mechanization of our spelling and of our speech. Our spelling is now written for the delight of the eye, and our pronunciation is for the delight of the ear. Uniformity in the first would be fatal, and the standardization of the latter would exclude the variety of beautiful speech. (*NA*, 13, 234, 1913.)

In the midst of his trivial relations of his trivial observations among trivial people, Mr. George Moore in *The English Review* makes one remark the discussion of which might be useful. 'The source,' he says, 'from which language is refreshed—rural English—is being destroyed by Council Schools; and God help the writer who puts pen to paper in fifty years' time.' I do not agree with either of the implied propositions, but I do not deny that there is something to be said for them. The sources of literature in the dialect are indeed in danger of drying up, if they are not dried up already; the great *Dialect Dictionary* has, in fact, as good as reported on the post-mortem of local variations. But on the other hand, the colloquial is always with us and offers the prospect of a boundless reciprocity with literary language. Admitting for the sake of the argument that literary language is the synthesis of dialects, its perfection is only possible when these have been assimilated and in their turn restored to common colloquial currency. Literature, so to say, takes up dialect and, after using it, restores it to speech in a purified and universal instead of local form. Thus the perfection of Greek was to be found, I should say, in Plato and Demosthenes, two of the simplest and most colloquial writers that ever lived. Swift in English is often indistinguishable from careful conversation; and, generally, style becomes perfect as it becomes natural—that is, colloquial. Thus the future of the writer is not the gloomy one foreseen by Mr. George Moore, for there can scarcely be an end to the perfectibility of language in simplicity. It is, on the contrary, a future of infinite attraction. Only when some writer arises as simple and yet as profound as Plato, or as simple and yet as impassioned as Demosthenes, shall I begin to feel any apprehension of the approaching surcease of literary progress. (*NA*, 14, 498, 1914.)

Correct grammar is a phrase that has the same meaning as the phrase correct painting, or correct dancing. In other words, if not actually self-contradictory (and in theory it is even that) it contains a misnomer; for grammar is not primarily correct or incorrect, but good or bad. Thus it is possible that grammar may be correct and bad, and incorrect and good. In fact, though I cannot quote Dr. Jespersen [author of *Chapters on English*] for the assertion, we can say that good grammar has developed at the expense of correctitude. Certainly, if it be the case, as everybody agrees, that the grammar of a language develops by idiom, we cannot fail to observe that many idioms are 'grammatically' erroneous. Logic and idiom are anything but always on good terms.

The transformations of the case-endings of our pronouns are particularly illuminating; and Dr. Jespersen devotes a considerable portion of his treatise to them. To be logically correct, the pronoun, as you know, must take the case-ending proper to its logical situation in the sentence in which it occurs. After an intransitive verb, for example, it must be in the nominative case, and after a transitive verb or a preposition it must be in the accusative (or, as it was called when I went to school, the objective). But does good grammar always obey these correct rules? Not by any means. For quite other considerations than those of logic enter into the actual products of grammar, and result, at times, in ignoring the logic altogether. Take an instance from Thackeray: 'It's not *me* I'm anxious about.' Correctness would require that for 'me' the word 'I' be written, for 'me' is nominative after an intransitive verb. The 'me,' however, has here been determined by the following clause which is to be understood as saying that 'I am not anxious about me.' This is an example of what Dr. Jespersen calls modification by 'relative attraction.' The superior 'pull' of the sentence was in its tail; and the correct nominative of the pronoun was converted quite properly into a responsive accusative. . . .

The difficulties created by the conjunction masquerading as a preposition are endless; and it is never logic, but always good taste only, that can solve them. Byron wrote 'except I'; so did Meredith— 'everybody is to know him except I.' Hardy, on the other hand, wrote: 'Perhaps any woman would, except me.' What determines in these examples the use of the one or the other case of the pronoun, and which is 'correct'? The answer is that one must look to the whole meaning of the sentence, and that the 'correctness' lies in that rather than in the logic of the construction. I can see, very well, for instance, why Meredith wrote 'except I,' while Hardy wrote 'except me.' The one was writing comedy in which correct manners were essential; the other was writing tragedy, in which the suggestion of a care for correctitude would be fatal. Both, therefore, wrote good, that is to say, perfectly expressive, grammar.

I have not space to consider the other influences enumerated by Dr. Jespersen making for the rout of the correct in grammar—the influence of anacoluthia, the influence of neighbouring substantives, the influence of phonetics, the influence of the word-order, and so on. But they are all very interesting as illustrating the æsthetic contention that language is not a science but an art, an art, moreover, perpetually at work upon its material of words. The aim of language is expression; and as language develops it transforms its own rules, but always with the single end (mark well!) of more perfect and fuller expression. For one other example, however, I must find room, if only because the case is crucial. Is it good grammar to say or to write 'It's me,' when correct grammar demands 'It's I'? Latham, Ellis, Sweet, Alford and others are on the side of 'It's me'; the other authorities, including the first disagreeable person you meet, are against it. Dr. Jespersen, as a quite impartial person, leaves the matter undecided. I, for my part, have no difficulty in pronouncing for one or the other according to circumstances. 'It is I' is certainly occasionally not only correct but good grammar; and 'it is me' is no less certainly occasionally as good as it is incorrect. The criterion is expressiveness; and good taste alone can decide which is the more expressive form to employ. (*NA*, 23, 123, 1918.)

English Literature
and Literature in English

During his fifteen years as editor of *The New Age*, Orage published translations of works by Chekhov, Gorky, Anatole France, Stendhal, Dostoevsky, and of Medieval and Renaissance poetry. Nevertheless, he asserted the importance of linguistic boundaries as demarcations of sensibility and literary tradition, resisting, as did the Vorticists, the internationalism of contemporary art and literature. After his years in America, he conceded that there was a distinctively American literary style, and did not assert (as he had fifteen years earlier in discussing the Irish Literary Renaissance) that it should be evaluated in terms of the English literary tradition. While the gradual changes in his comments on this subject between 1913 and 1932 could be viewed as resulting from indecisiveness or inconsistency, it is more revealing to consider them in relation to the history of that period and the ambivalence about language and nationality that it has forced upon us.

M

38 Importing Literature (1913, 1915, 1920)

Many modern writers . . . would, as they say, 'import' the qualities of French, Italian, Russian and even Oriental literature, into our own with the notion of enriching it and of making a world, instead of a national, literature of it. But this desire to include in the national form the forms of other literatures is, at bottom, anarchism; and is bound to end in formlessness. (It usually begins in it!) It involves also an impudent disrespect not only for our own national genius but for the genius of other nations and races; it assumes that our genius is imperfect because it is peculiar, and it assumes that the genius of other nations can be borrowed. Finally its effect invariably is to produce, not a pure form of English literature, but a hybrid marked by incongruities repugnant to taste. (*NA*, 14, 208, 1913.)

If I may say so without chauvinism, England is historically preeminent in translation, not certainly in quantity, for there both Germany and France beat us; but in quality. The English Bible, of course, is the greatest triumph of prose in the world. There neither is nor ever will be a more glorious translation. But other translations are, in their degree, little less masterly. *The* Montaigne, for example, is as good to my mind as the original; and *the* Rabelais is even better. Jarvis' *Don Quixote*, too, disposes of any desire to learn Spanish for its better enjoyment; and I would not spend a month to read the *Arabian Nights* in the original after Lane. I am not, mind you, depreciating the learning of foreign languages for such as either must for efficiency or must from a spiritual necessity. Were there no students of foreign languages—born and made—we should have no perfect translations. But in my Utopia translators would form a special guild to undertake for the nation the importation into English of foreign works, leaving the rest of us content to become masters of our own language. Nothing will convince me that a man writes better for knowing other languages than his own. He may, it is true, learn from them to improve his style; but no more readily than he may learn to improve his style by confining his study to his own language. The way to perfect English is English.

There are several signs that a period of translation is close upon us, even if we are not actually in it. A literary period is indicated when, by an undesigned coincidence, numbers of independent minds find themselves under a common literary enthusiasm. At present there is no doubt that many minds are wholly engaged in translation—chiefly from the Russian and the French. . . . We should take advantage of the fortunate period and, while the tide is coming to the flood, demand more still of our translators. Now, for example, is the time to translate, once and for all, the anthology of French mediæval poetry. What publisher will undertake it? Now also is the time, perhaps, to translate finally the French romantic classics. A word to intelligent publishers, if they exist, should be sufficient.

Prose, on the other hand, is, I must say, less in the prevailing mood. I have looked at a pile of French and Russian translations recently; but the majority strike me as being very indifferently English. It needs, after all, something of a genius to translate prose, and publishers seem to fight shy of genius in prose as if prose were easier to translate than poetry. Let me say once more that prose is a rarer accomplishment in England than poetry. English prose is more difficult than English poetry. Anybody almost can turn a verse with the traditional forms of our English heritage in his mind. It may not *add* to poetry, but it will pass. But in prose imitation is parody and is not permissible as it is in poetry; and, on the other hand, an original yet English style is most difficult to come by. Ask yourself how many living English prose writers you could discover in an anonymous prose anthology designed to exclude tell-tale mannerisms. From the pure style alone, with no other aid to recognition, I doubt if more than two or three writers could be infallibly detected. We most of us write so much alike (excepting in matter!) that peas in a bushel are not more indistinguishable. But that is not the condition for good prose translation. To translate into the best current style is to produce a translation for an age but not for all time. I doubt, indeed, whether at present any prose translations, either of French or Russian, are appearing that will not need to be superseded within the next ten or twenty years. (*NA*, 17, 428, 1915.)

Some profound and excellent things were recently said by my colleague, Mr. [A. E. Randall], on the subject of imported foreign plays, of which we learn there are a great number to-day. 'Art is born of inspiration, not of curiosity,' he said; and, again, 'Art lives by what it produces, not by what it imports.' Very true and very important. At the same time, I cannot help thinking that it is better for a nation to 'import' art than to go without it altogether; and, in fact, that it is the *duty* of its critics to stimulate home-production by importing as many as possible of the best foreign models. That home-production may fail to find itself encouraged to the point of creation is perfectly possible; inspiration may continue to be wanting; but of the two states of no home-production and no imports and no home-production and imports, the latter, it appears to me, is to be preferred.

'Foreign' is a word that should be employed with in.creasing discrimination and, most of all, I think, by English writers I hope I should be the last to deny that there is an English genius the perfect flower of which we are still to see; it is so, I know, in literary style, perfect English, to my mind, having never yet been written. The point, however, is that nothing foreign ought to be alien to a race as universal in character and mentality as the English; and that, in the end, the perfection of the English genius is only possible in a spiritual synthesis of all the cultures of the world. Two tendencies, equal and opposite, are at work, indeed, in this direction, and have always been in English history. On the one side, we find an ever-present tendency towards cosmopolitanism, an excess of which would certainly result in the complete loss of essential national characteristics. On the other side, and usually balancing the first, we find an ever-present tendency towards insularity and æsthetic chauvinism, the excess of which would undoubtedly result in a caricature of the English genius—the development, that is to say, of idiosyncrasies in place of style. Somewhere between these two tendencies the critic of English art must fix his seat, I think, in order that his judgment may determine, as far as possible, the perfect resultant of the blend of opposites. It is a matter, too, of time as well as of forms of culture. Not only are not all times alike, but there is a time for import and a time for export and a time for 'protection'; but, equally, there is room for discrimination in the kind of art that may wisely be imported or exported. In general, we should import only what we need and export only what other nations need, and thus, in the old mediæval sense, traffic in treasure.

Thus guarded, I think myself that nothing but good can come of the greatest possible international commerce of the arts. We must remember, as Mr. [A. E. Randall] reminds us, that the development of a world-community is not only a duty, but a forecast of what is to be.

From this point of view I cannot sufficiently commend the far-sighted enterprise of the American *Dial* in commissioning Mr. Ezra Pound to procure the best European manuscripts for publication in America. Without a doubt there will be people in America who will protest that such imported goods cast a slur upon native American art and, in addition, threaten the bread and circuses of native American authors. They will furthermore observe that many of the imported goods are exotic in the worst sense of the word, exotic even in Europe (where Mr. Ezra Pound himself is somewhat of an exotic, being more Continental than European), and still more exotic by the time they have reached America. It takes all sorts of cultures, however, to make a culture; and, in my opinion, *The Dial*, under its present direction, is contributing more to the future of American culture than any other journal or institution in the United States. What does it matter, for the time being, that *The Dial* presents the appearance of a contemporary anthology of European literature and art, that it smells, to a certain extent, of the school and university? America ought to be at school to Europe; American writers have a great deal to learn of Europe before they can hope to become perfect American; and the open acknowledgment of *The Dial* that they are at school is the kind of confession that is supremely good for the soul. Years hence, perhaps a century hence, the schooling which *The Dial* is now attempting to impose upon America will bear fruit in an American culture. Exports may then begin to balance imports, as they certainly cannot, treasure for treasure, at this moment. (*NA*, 27, 319, 1920.)

39 The Irish Literary Renaissance
   (1917)

After Mr. Boyd's warning note on p. 398 of his *Ireland's Literary Renaissance*, I risk being taken up for trespass. 'The main purpose of the Literary Revival,' he says, 'has not been to contribute to English literature, but to create a national literature for Ireland. . . . The provincial Irishman is he who prefers to identify himself with the literary movement of another country than his own.' This, I take it, means that we who are readers and writers of English have no title to pass judgment upon the literary work of Ireland; and, again, that Irish writers who appeal to English readers are by that very fact provincialized. The standard of judgment for Irish writers, even though they write in English, is the standard of Irishmen in Ireland. What the latter like is good Irish literature; and what they do not like is merely English. But this turning of the tables upon English literature is a little more than I am prepared to sit under. My contention is that whatever is written in English is to be and may fairly be judged by the standards of English, though it should happen to be written by an Irishman, an Australian, a Canadian, or a Hindu. The facts that the language is English, the grammar English, the syntax English, the vocabulary English are enough, in my opinion, to warrant a judge of English in proceeding to pass sentence upon it.

This is not to say, of course, that there may not be in a localized English literature a particular flavour characteristic of the local genius. We know that, in fact, in several of the counties of England there are writings in dialect which, though English, appeal particularly and even exclusively to the Englishmen of those counties. Barnes, for example, will never be fully appreciated (for all his inclusion in the *Golden Treasury*) outside of Dorsetshire; and in Yorkshire and Lancashire there are dialect writers whose works are unintelligible in the South, at the same time that they delight everybody in their own counties. But it is certain that Mr. Boyd would claim more than a dialect-value for the writers of Ireland's Literary Renaissance. While modestly disclaiming comparison with writers in the classical English tradition, he nevertheless insists that the recent Irish school of writers have created a style of composition, both as to form and substance, which differs essentially from English literature, and is consequently not to be compared with it, but which yet is not to be compared with dialect. For my part, however, I cannot conceive what kind of literature written in English can be other than one of the two kinds named. Either, that is to say, it is English literature pure and simple with a special 'note'—Irish, for example, or Scots or Welsh—or it is dialect literature—literature, that is, in the idiom of a particular locality. And, as a matter of fact, the modern Anglo-Irish school of literature is both. On the one side, it is pure or classical English, which can be read by any Englishman without a thought of Ireland (I am referring, of course, to its form alone). And, on the other side, it contains dialect-writing or the idiom of the Irish which cannot be mistaken for anything else. . . .

Mr. Boyd's confusion (if I may thus speak of a respected colleague) arises, I believe, from the admixture of purely sentimental with purely critical considerations. To begin with, as an Irishman jealous of his nationality and ambitious for the renaissance of Ireland even more than for the renaissance of Irish literature, he is naturally desirous of showing that the Irish genius cannot be hid under the bushel of an imposed and alien language, but will break through the classical forms of English and create out of the broken moulds new forms for itself. It is an admirable aspiration, and Mr. Boyd is to be praised for possessing it. But may we not point out that the new forms, when once they are brought into being, are forms of English? Next, I conceive that Mr. Boyd has mistaken Irish substance for Irish form. Because—and it is indubitable—a school of Irish writers have drawn their inspiration from Gaelic rather than, let us say, from Scandinavian, Greek, and Latin sources, he has concluded that they must needs on that account differ essentially from the classical English writers. But are there no other schools deriving from other sources than any of these that yet make no claim to be anything but English? If a school of English writers should (O most happy thought!) derive their inspiration from the *Mahabharata*, would they be justified in acclaiming themselves Anglo-Indian? That Mr. Boyd's galaxy of Irish writers are more or less alike in drawing their light from ancient Irish sources I, of course, allow. They remain an English school nevertheless. Finally, I should say that Mr. Boyd has permitted himself the uncritical luxury of discriminating in favour of the Irish over every other form of local English dialect. It is a luxury, too; for I confess myself to a weakness for the peasant idiom which Dr. Douglas Hyde first wrote down and Synge perfected by art. But there are other dialects and local idioms, dear and pleasant-sounding to people familiar with them, which no less than Irish deserve to be written down and perfected. But no more ought the Irish than they to be regarded as other than an English dialect. They are satisfied with their status as local modes of English—why not the Irish mode as well? (*NA*, 20, 229–30, 1917.)

If I were an Irishman, I say to myself, I imagine that I should *tend* to look at things in much the same light as Mr. Boyd. Having had my own language virtually suppressed, and being compelled to speak and write in an alien tongue, charged with alien traditions, I should feel the inclination to bite my own tongue, and to curse myself for the very ease with which the conqueror's language came to me. And when works of my countrymen, written in this alien language, were claimed for the literature of my conqueror and employed to adorn the triumph of his conquest, my indignation would begin to rise like milk on the boil; and at any moment I might be over the brim and writing nonsense about Ireland's literary renaissance.

But feeling, even of this intense and ebullient quality, does not of necessity carry its own justification with it. The heart should always be in flames, but the duty of the head is to remain ice. And after long reflection, it appears to me—though I write, of course, as an Englishman—I should, I think, come to the conclusion that not only was the wrong irremediable, but that perhaps it might be turned to excellent account. After all, what distinguishes wisdom from folly but the ingenious use that wisdom makes of circumstances which folly cannot employ and only fruitlessly resents? Given that English, by whatever abominable means, has actually now become the predominant language in Ireland; and that nobody either hopes, or, in his heart, expects to see Gaelic generally revived as the normal speech of the country—the conclusion to be drawn is that, for better or worse (at the discretion of Irishmen), the future of Ireland is, if not politically with England, at any rate, from a literary point of view with English literature. Irish writing, by virtue of its use of the English language, is inseparable from English writing in general. Both nations, whether they like it or not, are bound by the genius of what has become their common tongue. And the more frankly Irish writers accept the fact that, since they do not write in Gaelic, they must write in English, and hence, form a part of English literature, the better for their literary judgment and literary style. . . . There is nothing to prevent the Irish from excelling the English in its use; and in these days, indeed, it is an easy task. But what a re-conquest would be involved in that—to take the language of the English and to better the instruction! Great Irishmen, moreover, are there to prove that a profound Irish national sentiment is not incompatible with a resolution to beat the English at their own tongue. Swift was at least as patriotic an Irishman as any modern Sinn Feiner; his *Drapier's Letters* in defence of Ireland were not only modelled on Demosthenes, but they had all the patriotic passion of the Phillipics; yet he wrote an English which, for simplicity, strength and purity, is the despair of English writers. Is it impossible that literary power such as his may precede the political power of Ireland's ambition; and ought not that possibility to be present in the Irish mind? (*NA*, 20, 326, 1917.)

It is not a major question, but it will soon be having at least a topical interest: is there an American literary style? I remember several centuries ago discussing with Mr. E. A. Boyd the question of an Irish style. I denied its existence and said that what Mr. Boyd mistook for an Irish style of English was the result of one or two mannerisms and an occasional haunting rhythm. Time, I think, has proved me right, even to Mr. Boyd. So far from there having been an Irish style there was not even the germ for it; and in despair of the conquest of English the younger Irish writers have been driven to Gaelic,—which only themselves will ever read. The Irish case, incidentally, is not in my opinion on all fours with the case for the use of Scots as a literary medium. Scots is Northern English and a complete and legitimate language. But for various accidents, Scots might easily have been our predominant speech instead of a dialect. It differs again from our county dialects in being common to a whole nation, and also in having a national literature, small but good, to its credit. The language in which Burns wrote will never die. On the contrary, I see quite a rich future for it—Hugh M'Diarmid (Mr. C. M. Grieve) is a living master of the new Scots school.

The case for the existence or, shall we say, the coming into existence of an American style of English, is, again, not on all fours with either the Irish or the Scots. Certainly American English is English; that is to say, it consists entirely of words included in the English dictionary,—as Scots does not. Certainly again, what is peculiar to it is more than a number of mannerisms, such as distinguished Anglo-Irish from common English. Its peculiarities, in fact, are much deeper than vocabulary or mannerisms, they are of the texture called style, the warp and woof of literature. Miss Storm Jameson, I think, was warm on the scent in her remark that Hemingway's style, for instance, is not European, having a 'violence and a sharpness' correspondent to the American character.

She added that his writing is 'full of tricks,' which, I think, was to confuse the description again. I am not prepared to define off-hand the American style of English which nevertheless I clearly see in formation. Violence, sharpness, trickiness, are only first impressions of it. The literary naturalist would have to begin with Emerson, take in Whitman, Oliver Wendell Holmes, George Ade, and then come down to O. Henry, the *American Mercury* and *The New Yorker* to see enough cloth to be sure of the pattern. And his final impression, I think, would be neither of violence nor sharpness nor trickery, but of a crowd moving at high speed under a terrific urge. One gets excited, breathless, but very, very soon exhausted from reading high-powered American English style; but a style it undoubtedly is that has never existed in our language before, and it is not a mere variant. (*NEW*, 1, 45, 1932.)

Style

'Don't underestimate Orage's lit/ crit/ it was NOT aimed at novel writing, French impressionist criteria, BUT in tradition from Sam Johnson, and towards expository prose, i.e. clarity of a different kind,' Pound wrote in a letter to me (20 June 1959). Orage would undoubtedly prefer to have Swift's name substituted for Dr. Johnson's, but in using the latter, Pound attempted to characterize the values implicit in Orage's literary criticism as well as the sources of his style.

The most noteworthy prose stylists of the twentieth century have been writers of fiction. Emulating the success of novelists and certain essayists, writers of expository prose have increasingly made use of techniques that add to the piquancy of their writing at the expense of its simplicity and clarity. Orage was an unabashed advocate of neo-classical virtues in prose. In his emphasis on impersonality, he goes beyond Eliot, suggesting that those who have original ideas can never succeed in writing the perfect prose expressive of the genius of the English language itself. Through precept, example, and editorial prerogative, Orage attempted to make *The New Age* a model of the qualities of style that he advocated.

41 Definitions and Types (1915, 1913, 1921, 1918)

'Rufus' of *The Leeds Weekly Citizen*, whose references to me appear, I believe, in a new feature in this issue, cannot escape my criticism by flattery. I have had my eye upon his literary causerie for some weeks and a fallacy recurs in it like a repeating decimal: it is that 'style' is a mere ornament with which 'matter' can very well dispense. Mr. Shaw has been more responsible than anybody else for this particular falsism; it will be remembered what scorn he expressed for the 'literary professionalism called style.' But style, my dear 'Rufus,' is not something added extraneously to matter, like paint to wood; it is rather the polish that brings out the grain. To write in good style is to present matter in good form; so far from an ornament, it is merely the perfection of utility. What, no doubt, 'Rufus' and others have in mind is style in the manner, let us say, of Pater or of the writers of *The Gypsy*—style, that is, without any matter at all. For words *can* be prettily arranged without content, just as wickerwork—to take an instance—can be made without forming a basket. But as a basket is to my mind one of the most æsthetic objects, and mere wickerwork one of the least, so an arrangement of words with no utility only serves as a contrast to the beauty of words when arranged to carry matter. Style, once more, is the arrangement of words best designed to convey the matter. Let us hear no more of the quarrel between them. (*NA*, 17, 229, 1915. *The Gypsy*, 1915–16, edited by Henry Savage, attempted to revive the styles and themes of the decadents.)

The letter by 'A. E.,' reprinted in last week's issue of *The New Age*, is worth as much study for its style as for its ideas. In fact, when I read contemptuous references in the Socialist press to the trouble taken by certain propagandists with their literary style, implying that the time spent upon style is a luxurious waste, I am tempted to reply that style and idea are inseparable. You cannot be sure that the idea is clear until the style in which it is expressed is pure. Bad style is feeble or corrupt thought. The opening sentence of 'A. E.'s' letter is—I will not say a model, for that would indicate a sentence to be imitated—but an example of the adaptation of words to ideas. Read it aloud, and see how surely the voice chimes in with the seriousness of the subject and the style. I cannot imagine it being read except as it was written, for it is a genuine utterance. Shall I be told, on the one hand, that analysis proves the sentence to be most carefully constructed—perhaps written and re-written a score of times; or, on the other hand, that it is spontaneous and unpremeditated? I care for none of these things. *How* men write, the technique (as the apprentices call it), the idiosyncrasies of the author's workroom, are of no concern. What matters is that when a sentence is completed it is a living organism, as simple as life and at the same time as complex. (*NA*, 13, 761, 1913.)

There is as much difference between writing as an art and writing as a means of utilitarian communication as between painting a picture and a door. Art includes utility, but it also transcends utility. Over and above the desire to communicate thought there is for the artist as writer the desire to make it prevail in the minds of others; in short, art is a means of power. I should say that the end of the writer is to be able to produce by means of written words *any* effect he desires in the minds of others. To express himself is not enough; he wishes to impress himself; and words are the instruments of his magic. That this desire to subject other minds to his own is really the motive of the writer as artist is proved by the natural suspicion in which most writers who threaten to become successful are held by their first readers. Readers feel towards him the repulsion as well as the attraction of the snake for the bird. Power, they instinctively feel, is there, and they are afraid of it. Now style is only the device adopted by great writers to make their power more attractive than repulsive: style is power made gracious. I am sure that this, at any rate, is a more alluring conception of the literary art than that described in the volume under discussion. The 'don'ts' become easier to observe when it is seen that the forbidden qualities merely reduce the power of words. (*NA*, 18, 13, 1915.)

It is not the meaning of the *words* that counts for immortality, but the meaning of the *style*. Style, we may say, is a kind of supermeaning. In great writing there is always a temporal and an eternal value. Its temporal message is for its day, and is conveyed in the vocabulary and the facts of the moment; its eternal message is for humanity stretched upon all time, and is conveyed in the style. That Milton's pamphlets are 'unreadable' to his present posterity is no slight upon them, but upon us. We have lost the taste for style—above all, for the grand style. Yet of all the English writers it is Milton we need most to-day. (*NA*, 16, 566, 1915.)

It says very little for literary criticism, both in France and in England, that people should still be concerned about the 'style' of Stendhal. Stendhal had no style. Like Carlyle and others who aimed at integral self-expression, he had his own way of saying things, a personal manner; but style, in the strict and proper sense of approximation to the perfect *norm* of language scarcely entered Stendhal's consciousness. There are, to my mind, two classes of writers, both of whom may be great. One class succeeds by the achievement of perfect personal self-expression; the other by the perfect impersonal expression of the genius of the language. And only the latter can be regarded as stylists. Whatever is idiosyncratic, betraying the peculiarities, even if they be virtues, of the actual writer, is excluded from the conception of style; for style, I repeat, is inherent in the language and not in the character of the writer. The business of the stylist is to get himself out of the way and to let the genius of the language speak through him. The other sort of writer, on the contrary, must subordinate the genius of the language to himself and employ language instead of being employed by it. Stendhal, it is obvious, belongs to this latter class. In spite of all his appearance of objectivism—cultivated as compensation for his temperamental romanticism—yes, I say it after re-reading *De l'Amour*; his temperamental romanticism, in spite of his declared aim of writing in the style of the French Civil Code—Stendhal actually wrote in a script peculiar to himself. It was anything but the 'perfect civil service caligraphy' at which the first class of writers aim; but it was a 'fist' unique. The barbarous terminology will be excused, I hope, on account of its clarity.

The two types of writer just described are radically different as well as different in mode of expression. It is a question of real originality. Carlyle could not, if he had tried all his life, write in perfect English style. Of nothing that he could write would it be possible to say, 'There speaks the natural voice of the genius of the English language.' All that one could say would be: 'That is the authentic voice of Carlyle.' And it was the same with Stendhal and French. Nobody who, like Stendhal, could describe 'thinking as you read' as being an act of intelligence '*in defiance* of nature' (a profoundly true remark) could be content to write academy French. Academy French, like academy or classical English, forbids the intrusion into the writer's mind of new and startling truths. I do not say, of course, that a perfect French or English style must be confined to commonplaces; it is, however, confined to what may be called the extraordinarily ordinary; whereas the other kind of expression is only tolerable to the degree that it contains extraordinary and individual perceptions, such as the one just quoted from Stendhal. The observation is important as a guide to young writers as well as to literary critics; for the test to apply to oneself and others, in respect of style, is the possession of real originality. Have you ever thought a new thought—your appointed expression is personal. Are your thoughts only elaborations or what not of common thoughts—you may succeed in writing classical English or French or whatever may be your native language. Your literary horoscope, in fact, is cast by the quality of your mind; and it is best that it be followed. Stendhal made a great mistake in ever trying to write French. He thereby not only failed to write French, but he never quite succeeded in writing Stendhalese. (*NA*, 29, 20, 1921.)

[A correspondent,] in a perhaps chastening spirit, copies out for me de Quincey's 'fine analysis of Swift's style'—as follows:

> The main qualification for such a style was plain good sense, natural feeling, unpretendingness, some little scholarly practice in the putting together of sentences so as to avoid mechanical awkwardness of construction, but, above all, the advantage of a *subject* such in its nature as instinctively to reject ornament lest it should draw attention from itself. Such subjects are common; but grand impassioned subjects insist upon a different treatment; and there it is that the true difficulties of style commence, and there it is that your worshipful Master Jonathan would have broken down irrecoverably.

This 'fine analysis' of Swift's style does not appear to me to be anything more than a powerful attack delivered by an apostle of the opposing school. Swift and de Quincey are obviously poles apart in the direction of their style. . . . At bottom the controversy carries us back to the very foundations of European culture; and if I should say that, on the whole, Swift followed the Greek tradition—exemplified by Demosthenes—while de Quincey followed the Latin—exemplified by Cicero—the discussion will be realized as only just beginning. There can be no doubt of the school to which Swift belonged; his *Drapier's Letters*, for instance, were confessedly modelled on Demosthenes. Likewise there can be no doubt of the school which de Quincey attended: he learned his style of Cicero. The question, however, is one of taste; by no means a matter *non est disputandem*. Which of the two schools of style is capable of the highest absolute development; and, above all, which is the most suited to the English language? As for me, my mind is fully made up; I am for the Greek and Demosthenes against the Latin and Cicero. I am for Swift against de Quincey; for the simple against the ornate.

De Quincey appears to me to fall into an almost vulgar error in assuming that the style of plain good sense cultivated by Swift is fit only for commonplace subjects; and that 'grand impassioned subjects' demand an ornate style. In the first place, the style of Demosthenes was obviously quite as well fitted to the high subject of his 'Discourse on the Crown' as to the details for the fitting out of an expedition against Philip. The *Apology* of Plato is in much the same style, and not even de Quincey would say that the subject was not anything but commonplace. And, secondly, with the majority of English critics, I have a horror of fine writing and *especially* about fine things. The proper rule, it appears to me, is the very reverse of that laid down by de Quincey: it is on no account to write upon 'grand impassioned subjects' in a grand impassioned style. After all, as the Greeks understood, there are an infinite number of degrees of simplicity; ranging from the simple colloquial to the simple grand. The ornate Latin style, with *its* degrees of ornateness, is, on the other hand, a bastard style, fit only for—well, well, we need not discuss it. At any rate, the conclusion seems to me to be this: that the simple style is capable of anything, even of dealing with 'grand impassioned subjects'; whereas the ornate style is only barely tolerable in the most exceptional circumstances. I would sooner trust Swift than de Quincey not to embarrass a reader on a difficult occasion; as, for the same reason, I prefer Shakespeare the Greek to Ben Jonson the Latinist. We are, perhaps, returning to an era when the choice between the two traditions is again to be made; between the infinitely simple and the infinitely ornate. My vote is for the simple. (*NA*, 23, 351–2, 1918.)

A delectable task awaits a favoured man, that of collating, extracting and presenting in a single treatise all the valuable elements contained in the hundred and one books upon literary style and composition. As my readers know, I have a ravenous appetite for books of this kind; and still I have by no means read all that have been published even recently. No, not by a score that I could name, among them having been until last week, if you will believe me, Stevenson's *Art of Writing*. Having now read it, however, I am able to say that it certainly contains, along with a number of surprising misunderstandings, one or two fragmentary observations fit for the Final Treatise of my imagination. For instance, upon style in its craft-aspect Stevenson said what in my judgment is both original and true, namely, that it is the one essential quality of writing in which deliberate self-improvement is always possible. Other essential qualities of writing are, as it were, gifts of nature and experience; but the perfection of a personal style is a work of art, or, if I may play on the phrase, the art of work. From this point of view, or, rather, with this criterion, we ought to be able to apply a scientific stylometry to literature in general, and to classify periods both in respect of schools and of indidividuals with the accuracy of connoisseurs. Shakespeare, for instance—but I must not touch on that subject for another week or two; you are tired of it. . . .

In his account of the nature of prose Stevenson lamentably failed to be anything more than negative and superficial. Apparently, his only conception of the rhythm of prose was that it should not be the rhythm of verse. 'It may be anything,' he says, 'but it must not be verse.' Curiously enough, upon the very page upon which Stevenson says this of prose, he himself falls into blank verse unconsciously:

> but for that very reason word is linked
> suggest no measure but the one in hand
> one following another will produce.

And on turning over the same prose essay I find him lapsing into blank verse on, at least, another score of occasions. So much for precept and example. But Stevenson was surely wrong in regarding prose as merely not-verse; and, again, when he says that 'the rule of rhythm in prose is not so *intricate*' as the rule in verse. It is not regular, of course; and it is, therefore, not so obvious. In fact, Stevenson was right when he said that the rhythm of prose should never be as obvious as the rhythm of verse. But that it is less intricate on this account is the very reverse of the truth; it is far more intricate. Having for many years written no verse myself, I am perhaps a little jealous for the fair fame of prose. I resent the insinuation of the verse-makers that verse is more difficult, more honourable, or more beautiful than prose. In my judgment, a perfect prose is the last word in literature, since it contains every kind of rhythm to be found in verse, and other rhythms as well, and all in such a rich variety and seeming irregularity that while no rhythm is insistent every rhythm is heard. Verse is a solo, a melody; it is, if you like, something even more elaborate, a harmony of chords, a sonata, a composition for the organ; but it is always, to my mind, played upon a single instrument. Prose, on the other hand, is an orchestra, consisting not only of all the instruments on which verse can be played, but of instruments unanswerable to verse. Where in verse will you find the foot of more than, at most, four syllables? And even these quadrupeds (the antispast, choriamb, di-iamb, dispondee, etc.), can rarely be made to dance in a measure. But in prose, not only have we the use of the two-, the three-, and the four-syllabled feet, but the five- (the dochmiac) and the six-syllabled as well. The craft of prose is the employment of these rhythms without the appearance of rhythm. Their very variety makes it possible to disguise their individual existence. They mix and mingle in such rapid succession that the reader can never be aware of one more than of another. It is the charm of the rhythm of prose that it steals upon the senses without detection. To say, therefore, that the rhythm of prose is less intricate than the rhythm of verse is the triumph of prose over criticism. Prose laughs at Stevenson while he says it; and, in revenge, trips him up with his blank lines to prove how much more easily verse may be written than prose. I wish Stevenson were alive to hear what prose thinks of him. He was an honest craftsman, and I think he would have enjoyed being corrected for his improvement. (*NA*, 21, 267, 1917.)

43 Examples of English Prose: Milton, Chesterton, and Belloc (1916, 1918, 1915)

By chance the other day I picked up a complete edition of the prose works of Milton (why are they not in Dent's 'Everyman Series'?) and read for the first time his *Apology for Smectymnuus*. I expected to be shocked by the violence of his polemic, for which, as we know, everybody seems to owe an apology but Milton. I was, however, shocked not by the violence of his language, but by the feebleness of his reasoning. Bishop Hale must indeed have had a triumph! Milton, it must be remembered, was on trial, as it were, for both his own reputation and for the reputation of the cause espoused by the five men whose initials form the word Smectymnuus. He had, therefore, every reason to be on his most persuasive and forcible behaviour. Yet we find him dragging into his treatise long and tedious accounts of himself, of his early education, of his disposition and habits, as if Bishop Hall cared in the least degree about the truth of these things. Hall's innuendoes Milton took seriously, being, as he was, entirely devoid of humour. But there is something worse than a lack of humour in Milton's Apologia: there is a total inability to realize the state of mind of his judge and jury. Read, if you will, Demosthenes' 'Oration on the Crown' in which he defended himself for his life. Remark that, like Milton, he had to give a personal as well as a public account of himself. But see how persuasively he does it, as if every word he spoke were in danger of procuring his ostracism (as, indeed, it was!). You may not—as I do—admire the cunning of the orator as he felt his way into the minds of his hearers and finally established himself there to the discomfiture of Æschines. But you must admit that, for what it was, an Apology and a justification of himself, nothing could be conceived more exquisitely adapted to its end. Milton, on the other hand, seems, as I have said, to have had no sympathetic understanding, even for a cunning purpose, of the mind either of his antagonist or of his readers. The former he most certainly did not convince; and I much doubt whether a single reader, contemporary or subsequent, has been moved to agree with him. In this self-wrapped egotism he resembles Burke, who imitated him. Burke, too, would never, I think, have convinced any audience in the world. Most audiences, in fact, declined even to listen to him. Well, that is not oratory nor is it argument. And as controversy it is still less worth the name.

But this is not to say that Milton's *Apology*, like Burke's speeches, is not worth the reading, yes, and the re-reading and the close study. I rose from it with a poor opinion, it is true, of Milton's debating powers; but with a renewed sense of his immense energy. (Energy, energy—that reminds me that I have something to say one day of Stendhal's worship of energy, in which cult he misled Nietzsche.) Milton's energy communicates itself to the reader as an electric lamp is lit on contact with a dynamo. It is not what he says that matters in the least, but it is the style in which he says it. The sense is nothing, but the supersense is everything. I can well believe now what I have heard someone say, that foreigners ignorant of English, hearing Milton read, derive therefrom a conception of England more nearly the truth than any number of travellers' tales. (*NA*, 18, 470, 1916.)

Mr. Pound ... has been called over the coals for his impolite dismissal of Mr. G. K. Chesterton as one of the dangers of English literature. But, good gracious, Mr. G. K. Chesterton's reputation is not so frail that it cannot take care of itself against a spirited idiosyncrasy. Mr. Pound has expressed his honest opinion, and I, for one, do not wholly agree with him; but what is discussion for but to elicit opinions and then to extract the truth from them? There is undoubtedly a fragment of truth in Mr. Pound's view of Mr. G. K. Chesterton's influence. It is this: that Mr. Chesterton is a most dangerous man to imitate. His imitators really become apes. But that is not to say that Mr. Chesterton is not himself a great writer. Shakespeare is likewise a dangerous man to imitate; and we should only be repeating good criticism if we affirmed that the influence of Shakespeare upon English style has been on the whole bad. But this is not to detract from the greatness of Shakespeare. Every writer of a unique style is liable to ruin his imitators; and, from this point of view, the wise thing to be done is to classify good writers as writers to be imitated and writers never to be imitated. Among the former are the writers whom personally I prefer; for I love best the men of the eighteenth century who aimed at writing as nearly as possible like the world and through whom the common genius of the English language spoke. But there is pleasure and profit also in the highly individualized styles of the latter sort of writers, beginning, let us say, with 'Euphues' and represented to-day by Mr. G. K. Chesterton. Mr. Pound, it is true, may have no fancy for the unique and personally invented style of Mr. Chesterton; but it is a matter entirely of taste and not of judgment. Should he, on the other hand, announce that he cannot tolerate Swift or Burke or Milton, writers of pure English, then, indeed, I should join our correspondents in deploring his judgment. As it is, I listen to his remarks on Mr. Chesterton as I should hear his opinion of crab-soup. (*NA*, 22, 231–2, 1918.)

It is too late to expect Mr. G. K. Chesterton to change his style, or, rather, to adapt it to his subject; so it must be said, tout simplement, that the style of *The Crimes of England* is a deplorable misfit. In the tradition of literature there is an established rule that the matter and the manner must be somehow in harmony; and, moreover, the particular harmonies are by this time pretty well fixed as well. For instance, you would not expect to find an epic in limerick-metre; nor would you expect to find puns in a funeral oration. Mr. G. K. Chesterton has, however, one manner (I am speaking of his prose only), which he applies to every matter. Let the subject be naturally cheerful, fanciful, serious or tragic, the same style may confidently be looked for from him—and consequently the same result will be achieved. As an exhibition of Mr. Chesterton's miraculous cleverness, Mr. Chesterton's almost fanatical earnestness, Mr. Chesterton's knowledge and insight, *The Crimes of England* is, I venture to say, one of his two best works; but as an exposé of the crimes of England or, for the matter of that, of Germany either, it is unconvincing. The *truth* of what Mr. Chesterton says is the last thing the reader thinks about. So dazzled are we by the verbal sparklings of Mr. Chesterton's wit that it is as if we were trying to read by the light of fireworks; we can read nothing for the explosions and the coloured spectacles. Look, for example, at this passage, which is typical: 'Cobbett was defeated because the English people was defeated. After the frame-breaking riots, men, as men, were beaten: and machines, as machines, had beaten them. Peterloo was as much the defeat of the English as Waterloo was the defeat of the French. Ireland did not get Home Rule because England did not get it. Cobbett would not forcibly incorporate Ireland, least of all the corpse of Ireland.' Read one after the other in the ordinary way, they stun the mind like a series of shocks; no meaning can survive them. And, considered sentence by sentence, they scarcely repay the trouble.

Upon some fantastic subject such an intrusion of the oddities of the writer is no intrusion at all. Provided that the whole subject is one for cleverness, brilliance and literary fun, Mr. Chesterton's style is, indeed, made in heaven to suit it. But in a matter by no means of Mr. Chesterton's invention—namely, the war—and one in which the oddest of us ought to feel and act and think as uniformly as possible with our fellow-countrymen—the apparition of Mr. Chesterton in all his idiosyncracies is very nearly an impertinence. Matthew Arnold used to say that the business of the critic is to get himself out of the way of the author he wishes to present. However that may be—for it is not the whole truth—the business, certainly, of anybody who writes on public affairs at a time when they are really public is to write as if he were a scribe simply, and the public dictating: 'the hearts of all consenting to the voice of one.' It was in this 'common' style (as elevated, however, as the writer could rise in the 'common' mind) that Demosthenes and Lincoln delivered their orations, and Swift transcribed his *Conduct of the Allies*. True, the style still remained individual, unique; but it was, nevertheless, the style in which its readers would wish themselves to write if they could. Save for inevitable refraction the subject shone so clearly through it that the actual writer might easily have been overlooked— as he had overlooked himself while writing. Nobody, however, can forget in reading *The Crimes of England* that it is Mr. G. K. Chesterton and nobody else who is writing. His inversions and antitheses and paradoxes betray his presence as clearly (and as improperly to my mind) as the egoistic interludes of Mr. Bernard Shaw. Both, therefore, may profess as sincerely as they please that they write for England; but England writes for herself in neither of them.

I must except from these comments the dedicatory letter to 'Professor Whirlwind,' and the concluding chapter describing the Battle of the Marne. In the former, Mr. Chesterton has a particular person to address, and in the latter a dramatic historic episode to describe. In the one, he writes with restraint, powerfully and yet persuasively; in the other, his foot is on his native heath of vivid description, and the result is admirable. Mr. Shaw, likewise, is excellent in letters, open or otherwise. Long after his works have followed him, his letters will remain as examples of written debate.

In personal letters the 'I' direct or indirect is quite in place. (*NA*, 18, 157–8, 1915.)

Mr. Belloc once remarked in my hearing that he cheerfully expected the whole of his prose works to die with him, but he hoped one or two of his lyrics would survive in the English anthology of poetry. This modest opinion of his prose is not shared by the two young writers, Mr. Mandell and Mr. Edward Shanks . . . who have just collaborated in a study of Mr. Belloc. They say, indeed, of Mr. Belloc's prose that it is the best that has been written since Dryden. Usually, of course, these superlatives applied to living writers both appear to be and are ridiculous. Moreover, they bring their subject into undeserved ridicule as well. But I confess that my first impression when I came upon this judgment was not one of instant incredulity, but rather of doubt. Was it or was it not true, I asked myself. The question was, at any rate, worth thinking about. Resorting to my collection of Mr. Belloc's prose works, I turned it over and over to remind myself of the qualities his style contains. He undoubtedly possesses lucidity, strength, simplicity and charm— the four-square foundation of all great writing. But was his prose therefore great? Might it not, for all these excellent qualities, contain others that, if they did not cancel, at least counteracted them? And I believe, on reflection, that this is the case. To begin with, I do not discover any real originality in Mr. Belloc's prose style. Its simplicity and other above-mentioned qualities apart, in which he is in the great tradition of English writing, there remain certain qualities, not absolutely English, but borrowed from English writers. The best English style is original in the sense that it betrays no originality of the author, but seems to flow straight from the genius of the language itself; it is, in fact, aboriginal rather than what is commonly meant by original. Of such a style when it is written (and few have written it and none a great deal) the reader remarks to himself that there was, of course, no other way of writing: it appears to be rather a piece of nature than a work of art. But Mr. Belloc's style, as I have said, is not original in this high sense of the word, or only so in its texture; for he has woven into it devices of his own which themselves are adaptations of the devices (or, let us say, the mannerisms) of other writers.

As examples take the following passages which I have numbered for later reference:—

(1) Every man who has written a song can be certain he has done good; any man who has continually sung them can be certain he has lived and has communicated life to others. It is the best of all trades to make songs, and the second best to sing them.

(2) The silence of the interior wood was enhanced by a rare drip of water from the boughs that stood out straight and tangled I know not how far above me. Its gloom was rendered more tremendous by the half-light and lowering of the sky which the ceiling of branches concealed. Height, stillness, and a sort of expectancy controlled the memories of the place, and I passed silently and lightly between the high columns of the trees from night (as it seemed), through a kind of twilight, forward to a new night beyond. On every side the perspective of these bare, innumerable shafts, each standing apart in order, purple and fragrant, merged into recesses of distances where all light disappeared, yet as I advanced the slight gloaming still surrounded me, as did the stillness framed in the drip of water, and beneath my feet was the level carpet of the pine needles, deadening and making distant every tiny noise.

(3) When a man weighs anchor in a little ship or a large one he does a jolly thing! He cuts himself off, and he starts for freedom and for the change of things.

(4) Now a woman's wrath is a fearful thing, and all men fear it, for according to her love so will her vengeance be; and their love and their hate come quickly, but their hate lives longer than their love; and they will make play with love but not with hate.

Let us consider these passages—they are, of course, selected, I do not pretend otherwise—one by one. The first is an example of the adaptation of the mechanically cumulative method and of the dichotomous method singularized in English by, I think, Macaulay. You make one surprising statement, then another; and proceed in the next sentence to repeat them in summary. The trope is then complete. How common the trick is may be seen in current journalism, where it pervades all space. Raised to the greatest height of which it is capable and where it becomes a literary grotesque, it marks (and mars) the work of Mr. G. K. Chesterton. Depressed to serve the purposes of party polemics it becomes the child's rattle of the Press. Its defect as English prose is obvious; it is not born but made. It is not natural to the language, but an exotic transplanted from the text-books of pedantic rhetoricians. Number two is undistinguishable at first sight from Stevenson. His *Travels with a Donkey* are largely written in this style. Other turns suggest Conrad. But not some defects which neither of these writers would have passed: the accidental meaningless assonances of 'ceiling' and 'concealed,' 'light' and 'slight'; the repetition of 'a sort of' and 'a kind of'; the pleonasm of 'deadening' every 'tiny' noise. Number Three is an example of mock juvenility, not to say puerility. 'A little ship or a large one' is not simplicity, it is childishness; 'a jolly thing' is colloquial cant; and the three remaining phrases are trivial conversation or talking for the sake of talking. Number Four reads like a mediæval puzzle or an Elizabethan translation from Old French. It professes by its air to be steeped in wisdom; but when analyzed it turns out to be commonplace and probably not true. . . .

It is not to be denied, however, that Mr. Belloc is a sincere man, in earnest about his ideas, and a passionate lover of freedom, and, above all, a fighter. I do not greatly disagree with Mr. G. K. Chesterton, who says of Mr. Belloc that of all the men of our day he is the stoutest-hearted in the love and defence of common things. Of such common things as make up normal human life Mr. Shaw is critical and, in fact, sceptical. Mr. G. K. Chesterton can only love them after he has exaggerated them out of common recognition. Mr. Wells is ashamed of them. But Mr. Belloc loves and defends them for what they are. At the same time I do not feel that Mr. Belloc has this passion in a permanent or in a simple or in a great form. For he can from time to time forget it; and lose himself in some other pursuit. Compare his works, for example, with the works of Swift, of Milton, of Demosthenes, of Burke, even of Ruskin. There is a level of intensity in these that there is not in him. They had too serious a passion for their purpose and too reverent an attitude towards their medium of prose to forget the one or to play tricks with the other. When they wrote they wrote for their lives. But Mr. Belloc, it seems, writes for his living, for his own pleasure, for love of a fight—never for his life. The times are still susceptible of play; and life, which for the greatest is a continuous sacrament, is for him still rather jolly. (*NA*, 18, 493–4, 1916.)

44 Perfecting English Prose (1916, 1920, 1921)

In his Introduction to his translation of M. Alfred Loisy's essay on *The War and Religion*, Mr. Arthur Galton has, among some commonplace stuff about the war, an interesting note contrasting French and English styles. The French style he compares to the rapier (not for the first time!), and the English style to the battle-axe; each of which weapons, of course, has its own peculiar excellence. The comparison, as I say, is familiar; but Mr. Galton adds to it an appeal which I can never ignore—an appeal for the recovery into English prose of the excellences of the seventeenth and, still more, of the eighteenth century. Simplicity, strength, and common sense,—these, he says, were the qualities of eighteenth century prose; and if, without losing them, the grace of the seventeenth century prose could be added to them, what an instrument of great thought we should have in modern English! The belief, I know, is common that English is a perfected language because it is a fixed language. But the fixity of language is compatible with continued development; otherwise a fixed language would be a dead language. I declare, in fact, that the best English prose is still to be written; and, if I could, I would direct writers to aim at combining in their style simplicity, strength and grace. (*NA*, 18, 447, 1916.)

The peril of English style, I take it, lies in its very virtue, that of directness, and its fighting edges are to be found where the colloquial and the vernacular (or, let us say, the idiomatic) meet and mix. The English vernacular, I believe, is the most powerful and simple language that was ever written; but the danger always lies in wait for it of slipping into the English colloquial, which, by the same token, is one of the worst of languages. The difference between them is precisely the difference between Ariel and Caliban; indeed, I am not sure that Shakespeare had not this in mind when he dreamed his myth. Caliban is a direct enough creature to be English, and there are writers who imagine his style to be the mirror of perfection. But Ariel is no less direct; he is only Caliban transformed and purified and become a thing of light. There is, of course, no rule for distinguishing between them; between, that is to say, the permissible and the forbidden use of the colloquial; for it is obvious that the vernacular may be and, at any rate, is finally derived from the colloquial. The decision rests with taste which alone can decide what of the colloquial shall be allowed to enter into the vernacular. In general, I should say, the criterion is grace; the hardest, the rarest, but the most exquisite of all the qualities of style. I hope one day to see English written in the vernacular, with all its strength and directness, but with grace added unto it. Newman, perhaps, was furthest of all writers on the way to it. But Newman did not always charm. Now I have written the word, I would substitute charm for grace, and say that the perfect English style, which nobody has yet written, will charm by its power. (*NA*, 26, 158–9, 1920.)

My old dream of the fearless English prose that has never yet been written has now invaded some mind on *The Times Literary Supplement*. The coincidence of opinion and even of illustration between us would lead one to suspect 'copying,' if copying from *The New Age* were not above the dignity of Lord Northcliffe's secretaries; as it is, we need only call it remarkable. 'One dreams of a prose,' says our echo, 'that has never yet been written in English, though the language is made for it and there are minds not incapable of it, a prose dealing with the greatest things quietly and justly as men deal with them in their secret meditations. . . . The English Plato is still to be.' Alas, however, that *The Times* should be just a little misled; for the 'quiet' of meditation is not the real genius of the English language, and the emphasis in my phrase—I mean the phrase of *The Times*— 'English Plato,' should be on the word English. Greek Plato translated into English would not give us what we are seeking. What we need is Plato's mind. It is characteristic, moreover, this demand for quiet or, rather, quietism, in *The Times Literary Supplement*; since, on the whole, the 'Supplement' is about the deadest mouse in the world of journalism. Above all, it is suggested, writers must keep their voices low, speak in whispers, even, perhaps, a little under their breath as if in meditation, in case—well, in case of what? In case, I fancy, that Lord Northcliffe should be wakened from his sleep!

I ask my readers whether their experience does not confirm me. Is there not a *hush* in the *Literary Supplement* which is not the hush of reverence for literature but of fear and prudence? At least I am always aware of it myself and I think that few readers can miss it. . . .

This brings us to . . . the question whether the perfect English prose would deal with the highest things in the spirit of man's secret meditations. I do more than doubt it, I deny it as being absurd on its face. In the first place, secret meditation is incommunicably secret; it is thought without words, and disposed to poetry rather than prose. I suspect our writer really means rumination, in which case, however, he is no better off. In the second place, the genius of the language does not run easily in reverie, it is a language that loves action and life. It has few cloistered virtues, and to employ it for cloistered thought would be to use only one or two of its many stops, and those not the most characteristic. Lastly, I cannot but think that the choice of 'quietism' as the aim of perfect English prose is a sign of decadence, for it indicates the will to retire into oneself, and to cease to 'act' by means of words. The scene it calls up is familiar and bourgeois: a small circle of 'cultured' men weekending in a luxurious country house and confessing 'intimately' their literary weaknesses. It is the prevalent atmosphere of the *Literary Supplement* and *The Spectator*. It is essential that there be 'equality' between them, that none should presume to wish to inspire another to any 'new way of life,' that action, in short, should be excluded. Once granted these conditions of sterility, and the perfect prose, we are told, would emerge.

The rest of us, however, have, I am sure, a very different conception of the perfect English prose. The perfect English prose will be anything but a sedative after a full meal of action. It will be not only action itself, but the cause of action; and its deliberate aim will be to intensify and refine action and to raise action to the level of a fine art. Anything less than a real effect upon real people in a real world is beneath the dignity even of common prose. The very 'leaders' in the penny journals aim at leaving a mark upon events. Is the perfect prose to be without hope of posterity? On second thoughts, I shall withdraw Plato from the position of model, in which I put him. Plato, it is evident, is likely to be abused; without intending it, his mood, translated into English, appears to be compatible only with luxurious ease; he is read by modern

A Chronicle, 1911-21

It is commonly and truly said that journalism is ephemeral. Most of the events of a week are unlikely to be of enduring importance, and in discussions of journalism by critical historians, their suspicion that journalists write about things not worth writing about is often apparent. At the same time, however, critics have lamented the decline in the quality of book reviews and journalistic criticism in the twentieth century. Once the ephemeral is recognized as that which may be of importance in its own time, interesting and unexplored questions arise as to the characteristics of good literary journalism.

The following selections exemplify aspects of Orage's literary journalism inadequately represented in the preceding sections: his attempts to discern the symptomatic significance of admittedly trivial events, his resistance to currents of popular opinion, his assessments of the state of English culture and that of other nations, his sense of the direction in which culture was moving. One function of literary journalism suggested by these passages is that of testing the present by comparing it with the past; another is that of recognizing what is important when it occurs, rather than later. It is difficult to identify the qualities of mind by virtue of which these functions are well executed, and success in predicting the future of culture is more difficult to account for than failure. These selections evoke the historical contexts in which Orage's criticism was produced and serve as a reminder of the pressures to which critics and creative writers of the period were subject.

A Chronicle, 1911-21

Have you ever suffered from a feeling of being excessively self-conscious; have you ever wished yourself less self-analytic; have you ever wished you could act spontaneously, naturally, and without all the paraphernalia of premeditation, criticism and subsequent reflection? Have you, in short, been a modern? (2 July 1914, p. 204.)

1911

One cannot justly blame Philistines for treating artists with contumely. It is their nature. Despite all the cheap honours now being scattered among artists of a certain kind, the wealthy classes of England still look upon literary men as not much more than performing monkeys. Heliogabalus had a dish of nightingales' tongues, and the Popes of Rome, I am told, eat larks. The English plutocracy are similarly disposed to devour works of art as a relish, but with no more concern for artists than their prototypes for singing birds. Art for them is the *hors d'œuvres* or dessert of their banquets; and artists for them are at best an inferior order of chef. But why expect more of them? The days of Augustus and of the Medici are past. For Elizabeth we have the fifth George.

What, then, can artists do?

Diagnose the disease and face the facts first of all. The facts are that England is growing uglier, that the wealthy will not lift a finger to save it, and that if artists will not make themselves responsible for beauty nobody will. And the disease is simply ugliness. Doctors do not need to be dragooned into recognizing disease. Why should artists refuse to recognize that their particular form of health, namely, beauty, is fast disappearing? Yet many of them are still ostrich-minded enough to deny it! Here is England rapidly succumbing to barbarism under our very eyes. Our senses cry out under the torture of ugliness at every moment of the day. We cannot stir a yard, a mile, a hundred miles without encountering a new ugliness planted and growing or an old beauty withering or uprooted. Yet in face of this artists still go on denying that the disease is spreading, and all the time producing work which, to any eye that preserves its vision, grows weedier, more etiolated, and less beautiful with every decade. (8 September, p. 511.)

1913

Paris discovered D'Annunzio, while Italy was counting him second-rate. Paris discovered Tolstoy. Paris refuses to discover Shaw, and though Germany has long been attempting to pass him off on the world, the Latin nations everywhere decline to accept him. For what other city of letters could similar claims be made? Berlin may set the fashion for the Scandinavian and semi-Slav nations. London sets the tone for the Anglo-Saxon world. But Paris is still the literary arbiter of Europe. (26 June, p. 233.)

Within two hours of each other two much contrasted incidents occurred, one in France and one in England. In Paris President Poincaré presided at a meeting of the Société des Gens de Lettres, of which he is a member, and uttered these words: 'It is French literature that maintains the constant influence of France abroad.' In England at Knowsley Hall, the residence of Lord Derby, the King and Queen were entertained in the conservatory, which had been fitted up as a theatre in cream and sapphire blue, with a selection of the 'turns' of the music-halls. Mob at the top and mob below, as Nietzsche said. (17 July, p. 330.)

The appointment of Mr. Robert Bridges to the Laureateship concerns me no more than the office itself. If this office were not more or less of a national joke, one might be concerned to see it occupied by a man who confesses to being unable to enunciate the King's English. There is probably but one verse writer in England who would have taken the Laureateship seriously, namely, Mr. William Watson. (Mr. G. K. Chesterton, of course, would have taken it in jest and fulfilled its duties only in earnest—a combination as rare as misunderstood.) Mr. Watson would have loved the post and insisted upon the grandiose dignity of his place in the royal procession. Mr. Bridges will not give us anything nearly as picturesque a return for our money. If his influence should count for anything it must be for the worse, for the affected simplicity of his verse belongs amongst the foolish things that confound the wise. However, he is good enough for his day. (24 July, p. 361.)

Science is at its very dullest to-day. There are no good popular scientific writers, and the state of the whole subject is profoundly unattractive. I am not saying, of course, that discoveries are not being made; they are. But their character arouses none of the hopes associated with the scientific work of the nineteenth century. In those days the scientist was something of a prophet and had a message of hope for mankind. But the message has proved to be empty of inspiration; and all that science has done is to improve machinery and to depress man. Save to specialists and workmen on the make Science is to-day of no importance. (31 July, p. 393.)

Ah, Paris, Paris, where even the children speak French. Talking with an English poeticule who periodically spends his holidays in Paris and writes English with a French accent, he remarked that he 'could not read *The New Age*.' You should read it in French, I replied. The notion that Paris is a sort of literary Mecca, a journey to which 'saves' an author's style, is one of the superstitions of lower middle-class Englishmen (these include Americans). There is really, my friends, no salvation in geography. Paris, it is true, is the arbiter of European taste; but arbiters do not create! There is less literary creation, I should say, in Paris to-day than in any other capital city of the Western world. The specialties of Paris are novelties and criticism, and in both branches, as it happens, Paris is just now at its lowest. Practically there are no young literary critics in France to-day; and the literary novelties young Paris is producing are things to avoid. The best advice that can be given to young English writers is to shun Paris and to cease reading French. The best preparation for writing great English is living in England and reading, writing, and, above all, talking, English. (28 August, p. 513.)

What offences against literature the British Museum will have to answer for! I can never go into the library without feeling depressed by the number of people who have written and left their remains above ground to rot. Another sight to revolt the mind is the number of authors obviously engaged in preparing new works. The act of writing books, I think, is indecent, and ought to be forbidden in public. From the Museum have come, I dare swear, a good third of the new books now swarming from the publishers. Scarcely one in a score of them is of the least value. Students intent on mastery prefer the original sources; and the general reader is of no account. (18 September, p. 601.)

Others may write of the pride which they call the conceit of America, but I marvel more and more at America's servility. Her businessmen may, for all I know or care, think something of themselves, but such literary men as she possesses write as if they were ashamed of their country. I refer chiefly, of course, to American literary critics. *The New York Times Book Review* has already been mentioned in these columns, I think, for its crawling Europeanism—and its third-rate Europeanism at that. But no less prostrate are its contemporaries, *Current Opinion* and *The Literary Digest*. Style and ideas you would not think from the pages of these reviews were to be found in all America. They are only, apparently, to be found in the corners of London and Paris. Of course, I agree that Europe is riper in culture than America; but the reason is that Europe has traditions of criticism as well as of creation. Consequently, a handful of people in Europe can always be trusted to recognize a work of art when it appears and to see that it is preserved. But in America, I am driven to think, a work of art might appear and, but for some European critic, fail of any recognition. The critics there have their eyes so glued on Europe that America is invisible to them. (25 September, p. 633.)

I received an invitation to the dinner hastily scratched up in honour of Signor Marinetti the Futurist by a London committee; but I should as soon think of accepting it as of accepting an invitation to dine with Barnum's freaks. Decadence I have often defined as the substitution of the part for the whole; and in this sense Futurism is decadence in extremis. I know there is something to be said for Futurism and that it contains an intelligible idea. There is no rationalism to equal the rationalism of certain forms of lunacy. But what is sound in it already finds a place in good literature; but does good literature find any place in Futurism? I have read Signor Marinetti's 'poems,' I have looked at Signor Marinetti's 'pictures';

and I see in both a cell of a healthy organism swollen and overgrown to cover and kill the organism itself. (27 November, p. 113.)

In the *Figaro* M. André Beaunier has lately been discussing the future of literature, of literature, that is as an art. He deplores the fact that in Mr. Pound's France the authority of criticism has nearly disappeared. There is no longer an instinctive and recognized consensus of good taste embodied in the judgments of a group of critics, but decisions are left to be settled by votes, that is, by numbers. The Society of Men of Letters recently settled a dispute about taste by voting on it; and last week the Goncourt Academy awarded its prize after no fewer than eleven ballots. Ten members constitute the Committee of Selection, and it is amusing to learn that in the first ballot not one of them voted for the writer who ultimately secured the highest number of votes. The final result, in fact, was to give the prize to the competitor of the lowest common denominator. M. Beaunier fears with good reason that this method is far more likely to spread than to die; for it has apparently justice on its side, and certainly ease. No weighing of the evidence is necessary; one man's opinion counts for as much as another's; and arithmetic settles all. Yes, I can see the method spreading and not only in France! However, M. Beaunier is not inconsolable, since desperation saves him. There will be no literature, he says, to ballot on. The conditions of art (and here he supports one of my colleagues) are 'silence and solitude,' both of which no longer exist, in modern life. (18 December, p. 209.)

1914

I think if I were M. Bergson I should begin to recant my philosophy; for to the extent that it is pragmatic its disciples condemn it. His lectures at the Paris University are now so popular amongst the ladies that not only has he had to protest against the unbearable odours of perfume brought in by them, but on account of the crush of fashion and the rudeness of his audience to his colleagues he has now been compelled to alter the time of his lectures to an hour when ladies are at lunch. Things culminated last week when his audience, to ensure seats for *his* lecture, took up their places at the lecture by M. Leroy-Beaulieu who precedes him; and this they interrupted and, in fact, stopped, by chattering, wrangling and singing the Marseillaise. 'From a popular philosophy,' said Coleridge, 'Good Lord deliver us.' But the prayer should be reserved for a philosophy and a philosopher popular among women. (19 February, pp. 498–9.)

Something will have to be done to put the advertising touts into their old place of menial obscurity. What services they perform to society I have never been able to make out. That their fees (amounting in all sometimes to a hundred per cent. of the cost of the article advertised) are added to the price is, of course, obvious—and that is scarcely a public advantage! In addition, they most undoubtedly have the effect of clamouring down anything that is good and at the same time cheap. Yet nowadays they pose as public benefactors and, to crown all, as artists? Mr. T. J. Barratt, for instance, who raised the advertisement wastage of Pears' Soap from £80 per annum to £100,000, got quite a eulogy for his epitaph last week; and Sir William Lever at the Column Club the other day claimed that 'advertising was as much an art as that of the painter, the musician or the sculptor.' It is really not true! Even a little Cubist is in comparison with them a god. (7 May, p. 13.)

Pessimism and materialism are going out of fashion. Everywhere I hear reports of a new hopefulness in the most unlikely provinces of thought and even of thoughtlessness. From London, Ontario, a correspondent writes that the midnight has passed; everybody there is now curiously speculating on the new dawn (and, by the way, upon *The New Age* as well). In a chance company last week of half a dozen men—all of whom a year or two ago would have been hopeless materialists—only one clung to the old faithlessness, and he with humour. Even Mr. Wyndham Lewis (whose *Blast* is now due according to its time-fuse) assures us in *The New Weekly* that 'optimism is very permissible.' Oh, thanks, thanks! But let us take our wine like seasoned drinkers and in good company. Chief praise, with study, of Nietzsche who first whetted our jaded Victorian appetites; then to the more steady philosophers who engineered the road after him—usually, damn them, forgetting to whom the track was due. (11 June, p. 133.)

I will say nothing of the purport of the *Correspondence Respecting the European Crisis*, issued as a White-Book by the Government. No doubt diplomatically it is all that it ought to be. From a literary point of view, however, I feel that Sir Edward Grey has not distinguished our country except for an absence of taste. The reply to the 'infamous proposal,' for example, is matter-of-fact and rational and introduces the moral objection as one only of the reasons for declining it. I do not, of course, suggest that the moral factor was of much account to the diplomats themselves. After all, they know well what level their conversation usually dwells upon. But on this occasion Sir Edward Grey was writing for England; and all I can say is that if our Army fights as badly as Sir Edward Grey writes we are undone. . . . We naturally cannot command Miltons as our foreign correspondents. One, however, should certainly be living at this hour, for England has need of him. Read his *Letters of State*, written in the name of Parliament during the Administration of Oliver and Richard Cromwell. They were as great in style as England. (20 August, p. 373.)

It is strange how many people are discovering their contempt and at the same time displaying their ignorance of German culture. Not for a moment would I have it supposed that I hold German culture in very high esteem myself. Except for Nietzsche all Germany has not in my opinion produced a world-thinker since Heine. German thought has been too exclusively German thought to matter much outside its own borders. But to pronounce such a judgment, mild as it is, requires at least a passing acquaintance with the best that has been said and thought in modern Germany. How much profounder a study is necessary to justify the severe and brutal sentences passed on Germany by our chauvinists! Yet have they so fortified themselves? Not only Mr. Robert Blatchford has denounced German culture without having the means of comprehending it, but the Bishop of Carlisle has denounced it without taking even the pains to comprehend it. Both these writers—I suppose I must call them writers—commit an elementary blunder which reveals their ignorance and demonstrates their impertinence; both assume, the one (I think) in that cultured organ, the *Weekly Dispatch*, and the other in that cultured organ, the *Hibbert Journal*, that Nietzsche is at the bottom of the modern Prussianism of German thought and was actually the master and inspiration of Treitschke. Now considering that Nietzsche was more anti-Prussian by far than either Mr. Blatchford or the Bishop of Carlisle —both of whom, I gather, are in favour of conscription among other parts of the Prussian system—the first charge is absurd. And considering that Treitschke began his lectures at Leipsic when Nietzsche was still a boy of fifteen, the second charge is comic. But any stick, I suppose, is thought good enough to beat German culture with; even the stick of sheer downright ignorance. (15 October, p. 573.)

1915

It will be one of the marvels of our age, when posterity comes to discuss us, that in the midst of events of planetary magnitude writers can write and readers read interminable novels about nothing. (11 March, p. 509.)

1916

It is very difficult to sustain the labour of culture in these days. The external distractions are so many; and perhaps one is in doubt whether events without are not at present greater than any possible event within. But this doubt is heretical, for it cannot be so. The greatest events are still those that take place in our own soul. But how to re-assure ourselves of this and to proportion our attention on this scale. Of one thing we may be certain, that no effort is needed to keep external events before our minds. They are too much with us, late and soon. Another is no less certain, that all our efforts run no risk of overdoing our attention to culture. On the contrary, every effort at such a time is likely to be still very short of providing even a fair proportion of culture's due. I would recommend my readers, therefore, to strive with might and device to keep up their reading and thinking, their reflection and study, as well as it is heroically possible. Let us all do it together, for I confess that I am in need of my own exhortation. Everything invites one to scamp the work of intelligence nowadays, to be satisfied with half-truths, or with no truths at all, to become a journalist! But nothing is more fatal to culture than journalism. (27 January, p. 300.)

1917

Rightly or wrongly as succeeding centuries will show, we have regarded the two greatest movements of the moment—the war against militarism and the war against capitalism—as worth the devotion of whatever talents we may possess. Both of them are movements for affecting not one class or nation but the whole world, the whole of humanity. Both are planetary. It is with no sense of having deserted literature for something of less importance, therefore, that I for one confess a pre-occupation with the issue of these wars. On the other hand, I affirm a sense of enlargement, of liberation, of occupation with things greater for the moment even than literature. (6 December, p. 113.)

1918

Of all the new sciences, psycho-analysis is the most inviting. Its immediate practical applications in the hands of competent psycho-analysts are already considerable; but the field both of theory and of practice has scarcely begun as yet to be cultivated. The first results, as is only natural, are mainly therapeutic; but obviously the method and conclusions of psycho-analysis will prove to be applicable to education, history, religion, and to statesmanship in the very widest sense. Mr. Kenneth Richmond, who is acquainted with the literature of the subject, has already begun to apply its conclusions to practical education. Others have begun to apply them to history and religion. In course of time, some publicist is certain to apply them to the conduct of public affairs we call politics with results, I venture to say, that will surprise the empiricists of to-day by their accuracy and effectiveness. For, in essence, the problem of statesmanship and the problem of education are one with the problem of mental therapeutics as well as with the problem of psychology. All are equally concerned with the mind of man and with the characteristics of its activity; and hence the discovery of its peculiarities made by psycho-analysis is a discovery of use in every branch of human activity. I commend the subject and all the literature available upon it to my readers in the certainty that its study will repay them. The age before us is the age of psycho-analysis; and it behoves pioneers to be early afield. (31 January, p. 271.)

1919

There can be no doubt whatever that war is contemplated not only as a possibility, but as a high probability in the peace that is just about to be signed. Hatred and distrust of Germany are to be found in almost every line of the terms; and since upon a peace of hate it is impossible to build a peace of justice, the pillars of the present peace are certain to moulder and crumble away and to bring down war upon the world once more. (22 May, p. 53.)

That America is the country of the future is open to less doubt as a prophecy when the critic has made acquaintance with the new and renewed magazines now appearing in that country. A tone of provinciality still dominates a considerable part of the American literary press; but it is obvious that tremendous efforts are being made to recover or, let us say, to discover centrality. More and more, American literary editors are aiming to interest the world of readers rather than a mere province of them. I need scarcely say, of course, that the world of readers is not the same thing as a world of readers. A world of readers connotes large numbers, consisting chiefly of readers in search of amusement; but the world of readers consists of the few in every country who really read for their living, or, rather, for their lives. To appeal to the latter class is to be 'of the centre,' for the centre of every movement of life is not only the most vital, it is the smallest element of the whole. As I was saying, the most recent American literary journals appear to me to be endeavouring to become organs for this class of reader. It is not indicated more plainly in the fact that they are enlisting European writers than in the fact that their American contributors are writing to be read in Europe as well as in America. America, it appears, has begun to discover Europe. America, it appears, is on the way to absorb Europe. And in the course of a few generations, if the present American magazines may be taken as indicating direction, European writers will be as intelligible in America as in Europe; and, perhaps, more so.

Among the most encouraging of them is *The Dial*, a fortnightly review and topical miscellany published in New York. Since the war, *The Dial* has expanded considerably and of set purpose; and it is now one of the best of such periodicals in any part of the world, France and England not excepted. (12 June, p. 118.)

1921

I have not read, but some of my friends have, two recently published

German works that ought, I gather, to be translated and published over the whole English-speaking world. If they are anything as described, Spengler's *Decline of the West* and Keyserling's *Diary of Travel* are works of epoch-making importance from their originality of thought and tragedy of outlook. I use tragedy in its essential meaning of elevation. Anything dealing with men and affairs sub specie humanitatis is 'tragical,' whether it be, in the ordinary sense, optimistic or pessimistic. It is, in fact, not the conclusion nor even the mood but the plane of discourse that differentiates tragedy from comedy. Comedy deals only with men; tragedy deals with men as Man. Keyserling, I am told, has taken a philosopher's mind round the world and written an Odyssey of tragedy. . . . Spengler's *Decline of the West* is both tragical and pessimistic. He foresees the approaching end of Western civilization and regards it as being inevitable. That a German should have this opinion is not a matter of surprise; but I am astonished at the number of non-Germans who share it. (7 April, pp. 272–3.)

Bibliography

A complete bibliography of Orage's writings is to appear in the journal *English Literature in Transition, 1880–1920*. Entries for his literary columns will list the books and subjects discussed therein.

Orage is mentioned in many modern autobiographies; see especially S. G. Hobson, *Pilgrim to the Left*, London, 1938; Rowland Kenney, *Westering*, London, 1939; Edwin Muir, *An Autobiography*, London, 1954; Maurice B. Reckitt, *As It Happened*, London, 1941; Paul Selver, *Orage and the 'New Age' Circle*, London, 1959.

The issue of *The New English Weekly* for 15 November 1934 contains letters commemorating his career by friends, acquaintances, and authors whose works he published. In Carl Bechhofer-Roberts' novel *Let's Begin Again*, London, 1940, Orage is thinly disguised as Whitworth, A. E. Randall as Dawes, J. M. Kennedy as Harriman, and Miss Alice Marks as Miss Jones. In Paul Selvers' *Schooling*, London, 1924, Orage appears as Tillyard, A. E. Randall as H. E. Bassett, and Ezra Pound as Eli Peck. Orage described his editorship of *The New Age* in 'An Editor's Progress,' published in *Commonweal*, 3, 376–9, 402–4, 434–5, 456–7; and in *NA*, 38, 235–6, 246–7, 258, 271–2, 283–4, 295–6. The second edition of Philip Mairet's memoir *A. R. Orage*, New York, 1966, has a 'Reintroduction' containing some information that did not appear in the 1936 edition.

Orage's criticism is discussed briefly in 'A Commentary' by T. S. Eliot, *The Criterion*, 15, 260–4, 1935; and in Ezra Pound's 'In the Wounds (Memoriam A. R. Orage),' *The Criterion*, 14, 391–407, 1935. In *Nietzsche in England, 1890–1914*, Toronto, 1970, pp. 219–68, David S. Thatcher analyzes Nietzsche's influence on his thought; and Tom Gibbons relates him to the intellectual trends of his time in *Rooms in the Darwin Hotel*, Nedlands, 1973, pp. 98–126. Meticulous in their research, Thatcher and Gibbons provide valuable perspectives on Orage's criticism that differ from my own in *'The New Age' under Orage*, Manchester, 1967, pp. 108–17, 235–65. A less favorable account of Orage's career and writings than those listed above can be found in Samuel Hynes's *Edwardian Occasions*, London and New York, 1972, pp. 39–53.

Index